# Master Class

## PURSUING CHRIST
### THROUGH
## PERFORMING ARTS

### SANNE McCARTHY

*For Madison and Charity,*

*who more or less started the
whole thing*

# *Acknowledgments*

My love and thanks go to the first group of writers who told me to write, the editorial staff of *Inklings*, a Colorado arts and literary quarterly with which it was my delight to work nearly twenty years ago: Brad and Nancy Hicks, Scott and Joy Sawyer, Jo Kadlecek and David Noller. Jo and David were also the people who read and responded to the first rough draft of the book you hold in your hands.

Additionally, I have appreciation and gratitude for Jane Beal, her editorial skills and the gift of a new friendship; for Steve Taylor and Cherri Parks, for never ceasing to support and encourage this project; and for Janet Serfoss, whose computer skills and artistic eye saved me hours of frustration.

# *Endorsements*

"I will see to it that *Master Class* gets into the hands of friends in the world of theatre. Weaving her remarkable story throughout, with poetic wisdom and creative biblical discernment Sanne makes clear how telling God's story is the unique calling and opportunity of Christian actors. Although directed to Christians in the performing arts, *Master Class* got me thinking of how, without acting on stage, I could more fully tell God's story in my world. This book deserves wide reading."—Dr. Larry Crabb, psychologist, speaker, Bible teacher, author, and founder/director of New Way Ministries

"Sanne McCarthy gives *drama queen* a whole new definition. Don't miss this opportunity to get a veteran theater maven's acting clinic on paper. I've worked with her (on a script), enjoyed her directorial creativity (from the audience), and simply heard her wax eloquent on the craft. You won't get the truth about this marvelous art, Scripturally contextualized, from anyone more qualified."—Jerry B. Jenkins, novelist & biographer; owner, Christian Writers Guild

"Theatre for me has always been like walking through Narnia's wardrobe into a magical, moving adventure. Every play is a living story, and Sanne McCarthy has made her home there. Her *Master Class* is a compelling extension of her lifelong conversation with students and theatre fans alike: inviting, hospitable, wise and creative. Pull up a chair and enjoy the story." –Jo Kadlecek, journalist in residence at Gordon College and author of *Woman Overboard: How Passion Saved My Life*

"Sanne McCarthy's *Master Class* presents the reader with a compelling argument for seeing the theatre arts, particularly acting, as compatible with living out a vibrant Christian vocation. She presents her case through what often feels like a personal memoir, gracefully reflecting on her own spiritual journey, while at the same time providing a Biblical foundation for her conclusions. She raises many of the questions young Christian artists ask as they seek to serve Christ through the arts, and then she offers insightful answers based on personal and prayerful experience." –Douglas Briggs, Founder and Director Emeritus of the Los Angeles Film Studies Center of the Council for Christian Colleges & Universities; and former Chair, Department of Theatre, Bethel University, Saint Paul, MN

"I'm so grateful to Sanne for finally putting these words on paper. This is a concise, thoughtful prose on the exhilarating dance between theatre and Christian spirituality and their necessary union. These ideas come from decades of thought, study and practice tested on the stage. The young Christian actor will find much needed relief and courage here." — Paul Romig-Leavitt, Dramatic Director and Actor at *Dare 2 Share Ministries* and co-author of *Cue Lines*.

# Contents

# Introduction

*H*ope and fear snaked through her tightly held form—crossed legs, stiffly folded arms, clasped hands and wide, pleading eyes. She was seventeen, with a slight build—a curve-free zone—and a cascading mass of curly, electric, naturally red hair. She was from West Virginia and she had never been in a play: "I just *know* I can do this."

She was right. At the university where I teach, she knocked our socks off with her scholarship audition. Focused, edgy, *truthful*. We didn't tell her, of course; I mean, we said it was good and so forth, but we didn't tell her she was amazing. It wouldn't have been best for her to hear that yet.

We cast her in a major role in the first production she auditioned for as a freshman, enraging a couple of older students who, honestly, *would* have been cast if she hadn't shown up. That's theatre. It's hard to take, sometimes. She came to the first rehearsal not even knowing what the term "blocking" meant. Oh, glory. We were in for it! My stage manager—my warm, loving and *fabulous* stage manager—another older student, befriended her, teaching her the vocabulary of our craft as I guided her growth in the role. It was a lot for her, all at once. In the middle of the rehearsal process she came to my office, where I held her and prayed with her as she wept over the learning curve and the unkind criticisms of some who had not yet worked through their jealousy. Ours is not an easy profession—not even when you're very, very good. She was excellent in that production—and in others, of course. I was privileged to have many times of prayer with her, and many conversations about God and about acting.

She is out of school now. Before she left, I had the fun of acting with her in one of Denver's small, professional theatres. She is now married with children, and continuing to act professionally.

She is why I am writing this book. She—and perhaps you, assuming that you are a young Christian actor—a student or a professional. I am writing it because I believe that exploring story is an essential, God given part of human nature meant to be enjoyed to His glory. Teaching university theatre for more than fifteen years has repeatedly made me face two deep and painful questions asked by young Christian actors:

## 1) Is it o.k. for me to be an actor?

The larger Christian community has been suspicious of the arts for most of the history of Christianity. Great Christian artists may be recognized from time to time. Often these are composers, musicians. Handel. Bach. But performance arts, and particularly acting, have traditionally been considered *dis*-graceful, shameful. Even immoral. As a consequence, young Christians are warned away from the arts. They are also warned away by worried parents who are afraid they will not be able to make a proper living. These parents want their children to be happy and successful. In our society—unfortunately, even among Christians who should know better—both happiness and success are measured in terms of money.

Not much consideration is given to the possibility that acting may be a vocation to which one is called, as surely as one may be called to teaching, law, medicine or missions. I see the arts as part of man's response to God, as endeavors that can be pleasing to Him and bring Him glory.

## 2) Is it possible to pursue acting without violating my Christian convictions?

The theatre world is full of very secular people with very secular worldviews, which results in productions that could challenge your integrity. Of course, every person in every walk of life faces questions of integrity in the choices made. But the question seems heightened and broadcast in the field of acting. In addition, the secular artists with whom you work may have misinformed presumptions about you as a person of faith. It can get complicated.

But, yes, I believe it is possible to pursue acting without violating your Christian convictions. But to do so you have to have *real Christian convictions*. Acting is not a safe profession for a nominal Christian. If you want to pursue acting, while remaining Christian, you will have to pursue Christ with greater passion than you pursue acting. If you do that, your life will be filled with an astonishing richness of liveliness, including wealth of kinds you know about, and some you haven't imagined yet.

That's why I want to emphasize here the pursuit of Christ *and* the pursuit of acting.

6 Gifts: Holy spirit inspired, craftsmanship, ability, knowledge, intellegence, ability to teach.

Playwrites Structure:

Linear — the incedents of the plot are arranged sequential like

Cinematic — can have Flashbacks & Structure of plots not in same order as events

contextual — Example: the Private life of master Race — made of many small scenes w/ individual plots

Playwrites theme: Structure of Plot to communicate idea

# ONE
## Theatre and Story

*What is theatre, anyway? How does it relate to story? And are we supposed to be doing it?*

I always found bedtime a particularly good time for conversation with children—relaxed, unhurried, a time to find out what is truly on their minds and hearts. Laughter. Connection. Pools of depth and beauty. When my son Colin was perhaps eleven or twelve I tucked him in one night and was about to leave the room when he said wistfully, "I wish the *Chronicles of Narnia* were true." I turned and smiled, "They are true, Colin. That's why we read them. They just aren't factual." His face lit up.

I had never before put words to the thought, but that answer sprang without hesitation from the core of my being. The gospel of Mark says that Jesus spoke to the general public in parables, in stories. In fact, it says he didn't speak to them *any other way*. This is an astonishing statement and has caused me to look closely at the value of stories. Sometimes facts don't make any sense. They are so hard that we cannot receive them. Stories help us find the truth that is hidden by mere facts. Story was the leaven of my childhood.

Growing up in a small town in the San Joaquin Valley of California, only very occasionally did I get to explore story on stage. There were a few school plays and church pageants, and my mother was deeply involved in community theatre. So, when they needed a little girl, I had a good chance at it!

We moved three times while I was in high school, and my bent for theatre helped me make new friends each time. In Vallejo I won a community theatre "Oscar" one season for Best Bit Part—when I was fourteen! By the time we moved to San Francisco for my third year of high school, I was head over heels in love with acting, and stayed so for many years. I majored in theatre in college. The summer after my sophomore year I got my first, exciting, professional work. A friend called and said, "I'm directing in

Carmel Valley this summer and I just lost an actor. Can you come down?" Could I! So at nineteen I sailed away on Cloud Nine for a season of that magical, legendary world known as *summer stock*.

Summer stock and summer repertory theatre are great gifts in the lives of young American actors. Small companies that only operate in summer exist in vacation and resort areas all over the country. These sometimes bring in experienced performers for lead roles and offer internships to college students. The work required of interns varies from company to company. One may be expected to build sets, make costumes or props, or work in the box office—any or all of those in addition to performing. Interns play the chorus in musicals, the crowd scenes in large productions such as Shakespeare's plays (sometimes referred to in theatre slang as a "spear carrier"— whether or not there is an actual spear involved!). An intern may even have some lines of dialogue!

My friend, Richard, who earned his way acting professionally for most of his life on Broadway and in regional theatres, used to tell a joke when we were in college, and we would all bust up laughing every time he told it. It was only two lines: in a totally fake and crusty upper crust British accent he would say, "Madame, the Invisible Man is here." He would then answer, in Madame's affected voice, "Tell him I can't see him." That butler with his one line is the sort of role one may expect—nay, hope for—as a summer stock intern.

Summer stock companies do one show at a time. Perhaps Sunday evening the interns and technical personnel "strike" the current show—clear the set and put away or throw away sets, costumes, props, etc. Monday the next show has a technical and dress rehearsal in preparation for opening on Tuesday. Summer stock has a tight work schedule because it is seasonal. There are eight to twelve weeks of intense labor which also offer a priceless learning opportunity and lifelong memories.

The acting was fun! Living away from home for the first time was intoxicating. The relationships among the company were filled with intrigue and romance. And my best friend, who was working there for the summer, too, told me he had fallen in love—with another guy. It was the 60s. It was a difficult conversation because it was a topic no one spoke about. I was not Christian, nor did I have any other defined set of values. I soaked up all the newness with virtually no critical lens. It would be another thirteen years before I would hesitantly reach for and begin to find my frame of reference. I will speak more of this later.

Many summer companies work in repertory. This means they perform several different shows during a week. When I was twenty-two I went to Whitefish, Montana, with a company of actors from San Francisco. We were there all summer and our advertising slogan was, "Stay Four Days — See Four Plays."

We were a young company — in our teens and twenties — with a young director — in his thirties. We lived and ate and performed in a ski lodge which was available for its off season. The first week we built sets and finished rehearsing the first play, Noel Coward's *Hay Fever.* We were fortunate in that, all coming from San Francisco, we had been able to start rehearsals there. The second week we played *Hay Fever* at night and rehearsed William Gibson's *The Miracle Worker* during the day. The third week we alternated *Hay Fever* and *Miracle Worker* at night while during the day we rehearsed a musical, Sandy Wilson's *The Boy Friend*. The fourth week we alternated all three while we prepared *Half Heaven*, a new play written by our director, Paul Rebillot. After we opened that we lived up to our slogan of "Stay Four Days — See Four Plays!" Later in the summer we added several afternoon performances of a children's show, *The Elves and the Shoemaker*, which I believe Paul also wrote. We also swapped roles for the fun of it, rehearsing each cast fully and making the change when we felt ready. After we each had multiple roles ready, we were able to create different versions of each show's cast for our own entertainment as well as that of the audience!

We worked long, hard days and nights the first month, but once we had all the shows open we could sleep later and spend our afternoons riding the ski lift and enjoying Glacier National Park.

It was a glorious summer. Our pay was room and board plus seven dollars a week! On Saturday nights after the show, we would drive into neighboring Kalispell, fifteen miles away, with our worldly wealth burning a hole in our pockets. We spent half of it at Moose's Saloon, where they had free peanuts and expected everyone to toss the shells on the sawdust floor. Then we bought chewing gum and deodorant at the local drug store, and that pretty much took care of our paychecks! Sometimes there was enough for an ice cream cone on a hot afternoon later in the week.

As I look back, with more of my life behind me than before me, one of the amazing things about theatre is its staying power in my life. But as we are truly made in God's image, and insofar as the arts help us to create that image, how could it be otherwise? Theatre has been a strong thread in the weaving of my life. It is true I have been a legal secretary, short order cook and day care provider. But I have made a living on stage in America and Europe, and that has been the flavor of my life. Eventually, I began to understand why. Eventually, I began to catch on to the importance of story.

In my thirties I gave my life very intentionally to Christ. The next twenty years were dense with new experiences. I lost my marriage and a whole lot of weight. I finished a college degree, pursued increasingly deeper knowledge of Christ, and began a whole new career. In my fifties, as a college drama teacher—a

Christian teacher at a Christian college—I worried about theatre. There doesn't seem to be a whole lot about it in scripture. In Exodus God gives beautiful and detailed instructions regarding the furnishing and building of the sanctuary. I Kings describes the temple and palace built by Solomon. Names of craftsmen are given. Specific, individual portions of those constructions are painstakingly, intricately described with regard to materials and form. These are accounts of the creation of manmade visual arts—accounts that are held worthy of inclusion in scripture. Or take music and dance. Music is spoken of often and fully in Psalms and elsewhere—vocal and instrumental music.

1) The Levitical singers are honored: "Those who were musicians, heads of Levite families, stayed in the rooms of the temple and were exempt from other duties because they were responsible for the work day and night" (I Chronicles 9:33).

2) David danced before the ark of the covenant: "David, wearing a linen ephod, danced before the Lord with all his might" (2 Samuel 6:14).

3) The children of Israel sang and danced when they arrived on the far side of the Red Sea: "Then

Miriam the prophetess, Aaron's sister, took a tambourine in her hand, and all the women followed her with tambourines and dancing.

Miriam sang to them:

Sing to the Lord, for he is highly exalted.

The horse and its rider he hath hurled into the sea" (Exodus 15:20-21).

In looking for theatre, however, all I could find were a couple of strange references in Ezekiel, where he draws on a brick and lies on his side for days on end. Later, I began to see a connection between the storytelling of the prophet, Ezekiel, and the prophetic nature of storytelling at other times and places. Prophecy is defined as both "fortelling" and "forthtelling." It is not bound by fact, but it deals with truth, whether future or present. God speaks through story. Jesus spoke through story, and we speak through story. Perhaps for this very reason, Satan attacks story with heavy artillery.

Let's face it: the reputation of theatre hasn't been very stable through the years. Shortly after Christianity succeeded in becoming the state religion of the Roman Empire, theatre was firmly squelched.

That was because it was filled with lewdness and immorality, it worshipped false gods and mocked Christians. On top of that, the feeding of Christians to lions—for the entertainment of spectators!—was literal, not merely metaphoric.

Theatre enjoyed a time of refreshment in the late Middle Ages. The mystery and morality plays coming out of the Christian church at that time are breathtaking in their beauty and theological depth. Those plays were undertaken by the church, for teaching purposes. The people were not literate. There was no printing press. Cycles of plays were written and performed in major English cities—cycles dealing with scripture stories. They were written by the guilds, the labor unions of the time, with each guild taking on the story related to its own work and knowledge. For example, shipwrights would write and perform the story of Noah. Through those stories the people were taught the Bible and the structure of their faith, all under the watchful eye of the church. With the invention of the printing press and the spread of literacy, over time more voices entered the mix and began to elaborate, then clutter, then outshout the Christian voice. In today's pluralistic society, Christianity is again out of favor in many quarters, and theatre is put to many uses, given many voices. There are many stories in the world. God's own story is the only one that will make sense ultimately. Your story, my story—any story—is powerful in direct proportion to its truthful connection with God's story.

More than once I have had a conversation with an embarrassed and distressed freshman who crept into my office to say, "I love theatre. It's what I want to do with my life. But my father (or sister or pastor or teacher or auto mechanic) says if I really loved God I would do something useful with my life, like teaching, or missions, or youth work. I think I love God, but maybe they're right—maybe this is incredibly selfish. Maybe I have no business being here, majoring in theatre. But I can't think what else I would do. I'm a Christian, but I want to be an actor. Is that o.k.?"

One afternoon, after I had been teaching for several years and had several such conversations, I was sitting in my office, contemplating the matter. (One of the cool things about being a college professor—and, by the way, this is a line of work I came to late in life, *after* being an actor, singer, legal secretary, day care provider and short order cook—one of the cool things about being a college professor is that I get to contemplate on the clock. During working hours. It's actually an important part of the job.) So I was sitting there, thinking. And I thought, "What *is* theatre, anyway?" And it occurred to me that theatre is storytelling. This thought was followed by a medium length silence while I grasped a couple of the implications. Oh my goodness. Then no WONDER theatre isn't mentioned in scripture. Scripture IS story! God is the Grandaddy Storyteller of all time! I lost my breath. Suddenly, I had been fished out of the dirty back corner of the arts closet and swept downstage center into the dazzling light. Yes, Virginia, there *is* theatre. And God *did* start it. Humans have woven an intricate fabric through innumerable forms that we designate as theatre, but the original impulse pours from the storytelling nature of God himself.

David Mamet, the American playwright, screenwriter and director, says people come to the theatre to find Truth. According to him, it might be just about the last remaining place they have a shot at finding it in our society. And when they don't find it there, they go away disappointed. But they keep coming back. It's a hard habit to break, Mamet says. That makes me think of Greek theatre, where people packed their lunch and stayed all day. There was an altar, you know, in the middle of every Greek stage. If you take a theatre history class, we will tell you this. But then we soon and pretty smoothly move on to other things because, see, after all this time and some really impressive research, apparently nobody still exactly knows *why* there was an altar in the middle of the stage or what they exactly did with it. Altars are generally for worship. So, then, the Greeks may have had the wrong gods (a not unusual occurrence that can happen to any one of us and frequently does), but maybe they had the right idea about the relationship between God and Story. How can we get back to that? We have the right God. So perhaps what needs our attention is the place we give to story.

As Christians, we have the opportunity for a unique perspective on story. One reason we might want to live life as a Christian actor is found in words of Oswald Chambers, words written in a letter home when he was about twenty-two years old. He spoke of the necessity for the arts to be redeemed for Christ *by Christian artists*. He said it isn't up to pastors. Pastors, in fact, can't do it. It is not inconceivable that a person could be both a pastor and an artist. But a pastor who is not an artist does not have the tools for redeeming the arts, any more than an actor has the tools for leading a congregation. Pastors, according to Chambers, need to free the people from their fears and prejudices so that a proper relationship with the arts is possible. I consider that this is a difficult task in itself because of the years and strength of influence of both the enemy and the flesh in the arts. However, the arts, *surrendered to Christ,* have very different characteristics from unsurrendered arts. Some of those characteristics have yet to be discovered, even by Christian artists, and only artists can do the actual work of redemption because it takes place from the inside out, and only artists are inside the processes and products of art. Theatre is a form of storytelling, and we may be involved in it as surely as we are made in the image of God.

# TWO:
## *Art and Creativity*

*What is art? And what makes the arts important?*

*I*n the spring of 1967 I knew It Was Time. I put together a resume and bought 100 prints of an 8x10 glossy head shot and Prepared to Go Forth. Jerry and I were going together. Our plan was to leave San Francisco, drive to Reno and get married, and then drive to Seattle, where we hoped to audition for the Seattle Repertory Company. A couple of weeks before we were to leave, we were at a party one night. There was a girl there, Shirley, who needed a ride home and I said, "Oh, we can take you." She said, "You don't understand. I live in Kerrville, Texas." I looked at Jerry. He shrugged and smiled. "We'll take you," I said, "if you can wait two weeks."

When Jerry and Shirley and I got to Reno, we went to the home of my sister who lived there. "Don't get married in Reno," she said, "everybody does that. Let's go to Virginia City." So Jerry and I were married in Virginia City which, at least in those days, was peaceful, old fashioned and very pretty. We were pleased. Shirley went to my sister's for a couple of days while Jerry and I honeymooned, camping in the back of our Ford Econoline van. Then we drove Shirley from Reno to Kerrville—still on our way from San Francisco to Seattle!

After delivering Shirley, we said to one another, "Well, hey, what's the hurry? If they actually *hire* us in Seattle, who knows when we'll be this far east again? So let's go to Minneapolis and see Richard!" Richard worked for the Guthrie Theatre in Minneapolis, and while we were visiting him he said, "The Firehouse Theatre is hiring. Why don't you talk to them before you drive all the way to Seattle?" So we did. They hired us and we acted for a season with the Firehouse Theatre of Minneapolis.

The Firehouse was a theatre community with strong political and social sensibilities that were represented in their work. I had virtually no political sensibilities and only modest social ones. But I liked the people a lot.

God's blessings in my life have been bountiful, even in the years when I didn't know him—at least, not to talk to. The year we worked with the Firehouse happened to be the year they/we went to Europe. I have magical memories of April in Paris, waffles and whipped cream at an outdoor carnival in the south of France, feather beds in Arhus, Denmark, and listening to Cat Stevens albums in an upper flat in Copenhagen.

Audiences loved us. At one theatre, when we came back from a dinner break, there were so many people waiting in front of the theatre that we sneaked around back and climbed a fence to go in through the stage door. When the crowd saw what we were doing, they followed us at a dead run! We raced up the walk and through the door the stage manager slammed behind us just in time to avoid being mobbed! It was fun! The press reviewed us warmly, complimenting our political and social agenda as well as our artistry.

So why was I unhappy and restless when we got home to the States? Looking back now I think I really didn't know who I was—certainly not who I was in Christ. I didn't know why I was in theatre. God's glory would never have occurred to me. That summer, I quit the Firehouse and went to work in the inner city. The Firehouse, which had not met me aesthetically or spiritually, had awakened my political and social sensibilities. But I later returned to theatre. I was no good as a social worker—I was an actor!

All these years later I see that being an actor isn't just about being cast. A theatre company—a film company—has a purpose. As a Christian, as a human being, I have a purpose. Being a Christian artist further refines that purpose. These purposes all converge and *matter* when I am considering a certain project, a certain audition. If you are a Christian and you are an artist, you are a Christian artist. What makes you different from other artists is your commitment to Christ before self, before art. When humans create, we are seeking to reflect the image of God as creator. I do not mean that all artists are consciously seeking to reflect God's image. This is manifestly not the case. What I mean is that I believe there is something in human nature, placed there by God, that desires to create. That desire is an *imago dei,* an image of God. "So God created man in his own image, in the image of God he created him; male and female he created them" (Genesis 1:27). *Imago dei* can be a loaded term theologically, but I am using it simply here, as a not-very-theologically-educated lay person. There are two senses of the word *imago* that are particularly useful to our discussion. One has to do with *reflecting* an image, as in a mirror. "And we, who with unveiled faces reflect the Lord's glory, are being transformed into his likeness with ever-increasing glory, which comes from the Lord, who is the Spirit" (2 Corinthians 3:18). The Greek word used in this passage, *eikon,* translates as likeness, representation or resemblance.

Being turned into the image that we reflect brings us to the second meaning of image that I want us to consider, and that is the idea suggested by Genesis 1:27, where God makes us in his image. The Hebrew word is *tselem,* meaning a representative figure, especially an idol. It is the same word used in Exodus 20:4 where God forbids the Israelites to make images for the purpose of worshipping them.

So perhaps we are made as representative figures in God's likeness and, when we look at him long and faithfully, we become more and more truly like him. God is life, and worshipping him makes us alive. If we misuse our likeness to him to make idols in *our* image, or in the image of other created things, those idols can have no life, because only the spirit of God imparts life. If we look long and faithfully at these idols, perhaps we become more and more like them—more wooden, more stony, more lifeless.

Human creativity, of course, is not limited to those working in the arts. Creativity touches every realm of human endeavor, and comes in many forms—chairs, tables, penicillin and computer chips, to name a few. Everything man makes or does in some way reflects the image of God. *It is our nature to do so.* Now, because of our fallenness, we reflect God in imperfect and broken ways. But we do reflect him.

I am not here to knock brokenness. The poet, Don Becker, once pointed out to me that pure light is white. Every color we ever see is a result of the splintering of that light. The presence of *all* color in light results in white light. Colors appear through the prismatic shattering of that white light. That wasn't exactly *news* to me—I learned the basic facts in technical theatre classes—but I would have to say that in revisiting the thought in a broader context, it struck me rather forcefully. It is both sobering and comforting to realize that so much beauty can come from brokenness. In fact, apparently brokenness is *necessary* to produce some kinds of beauty.

Albert Camus, the French philosopher, said, "If the world were clear there would be no art." This idea suggests that art is a response to the world, rather than to God. It looks at art through a different lens, not acknowledging God but, instead, observing the artist's response to the chaos of the world around him. I might add that there is perhaps so much art because no amount of art and no particular work of art will ever bring us permanent clarity regarding the Things That Matter. Clarity exists, if at all, only in the moment of creation. But here is an interesting thing. One may think of the "moment of creation"—in painting, for example—as the moment the artist put paint to canvas. That is only one moment of creation. Later, when the painting is hanging somewhere, every time someone looks at it and actually engages with it, there comes another moment of creation—another potential moment for the revelation of what is true, for the reflection of an *imago dei* in the person looking.

This is an easier idea to understand relative to theatre than to painting. It is carelessly easy to ascribe artistry to a painting while it just exists. But theatre only exists in performance—in the action, the transaction, the energy exchange of the moment. Plays may possibly exist as literature. Possibly. It is debatable. We have been for so long committed to the power of literacy in our society that we thoughtlessly equate the written word with the performed word. Why on earth would we do this? No one mistakes a score for music. No one mistakes labanotation for dance. Why do we think a script is a play? We do, at least, recognize some difference in performance. Even there, though, we don't ascribe *enough* difference. I can never send you to see the play I saw last night. It will never exist again. When you see it tomorrow, there will be at least subtle, and possibly huge, differences because the audience is a completely new group of people whose energies will synthesize differently with those of the actors, changing the actors so that they even relate differently with one another. The same thing actually happens with paintings. Art is a form of communication, and what the spectator/auditor participant carries away from the experience is not merely what the artist has deliberately or inadvertently presented, but an altered consciousness as a result of an exchange of energies. Nor is our perception of that exchange of energies in any way static.

Postmodern theories of meaning suggest that meaning does not reside in word or gesture, but rather in the space between the sender and receiver of the word or gesture. That is, you speak a word to which you attribute a certain meaning, a meaning based on all the nuances of your personal life history. I hear the word from the midst of my own nuanced history and attribute my own meaning to the word. *For us*, then, according to this idea, the meaning of the word lies in the center between our two perceptions of it. If you use the word with someone else, her nuanced history will attribute a different meaning, shifting yet again the possibility for what the word can possibly mean to you. In the purest form of this theory, it is suggested that this is the *only* meaning—that there is no absolute meaning to anything, but only that which is attributed by our collective experience. We acknowledge the partial truth in this idea every time we choose a word or image carefully—as painter, playwright, or friend.

As Christians, though, we don't believe in such total instability of truth. As Christian artists we seek words and images that echo the meaning we have come to believe *is* absolute. But we are working with the same vocabulary as the rest of the population. We struggle for ways to attach uncommon meaning to common words and gestures.

If meaning is so fluid, then perhaps only God creates Christian art. Christian means Christ. Jesus Christ. The Way, the Truth and the Life. Thus, Christian art is Truth. As God sends the rain on the just and the unjust, and as he is no respecter of persons, so he pours out artistic gifting. Truth peers out from page, stage and canvas in places we have not expected, while sometimes eluding us where we most hoped to find it.

Madeleine L'Engle, in *Walking on Water,* speaks of Christian art as finding cosmos in chaos. She suggests that merely to reflect chaos back to the chaos around us is neither art nor Christian. I agree. It may be a sort of pre-Christian pre-art. After all, at one time the earth was a formless void and there was darkness over the deep. Maybe, struggling on our own (and in contemporary society we seem to do a great deal of struggling on our own), the very best we can do is to mirror back that chaos. Ah, but God's spirit hovered over the water—over the face of the deep. Right there, in the second verse of the first chapter of Genesis, we find the possibility for Christian art. Maybe Christian art—whether or not the artist is consciously Christian—is the deep impulse of the artist to reflect God's hovering spirit rather than reflecting the formless void—to reflect cosmos rather than chaos.

Like any other Christian, the Christian artist's assignment is to die to self. This can be a very confusing goal for a performer in contemporary western society. Stardom—often culturally assumed to be the ultimate performance success—seems, at least on the surface, to be more about self-aggrandizement than self-denial. The task of the intentionally Christian actor is to find actions, ways of conducting the artistic life, that allow us to get the self out of the way. When we are drawn to acting, we are often confused by what feels like a duality to us—the desire to do well something so public while at the same time having a strong awareness of Jesus' requirement that we lay down our lives. It is this torn feeling that leads to the timid question, "Is it o.k. to be an actor?"

There is an odd paradox in the dying to self of a Christian actor because our self is the medium through which we create. Musicians have instruments. Sculptors have wood, stone, clay—stuff. Actors have self. We *are* the artistic medium.

A few years ago, I was playing Mrs. Watts in *The Trip to Bountiful*. In notes a few nights before we opened, the director remarked, "And I know that the end of Act II will be there when you get in front of an audience. You're just saving it." My heart sank. Mrs. Watts breaks down emotionally at the end of Act II. I had been very low key in my approach to that moment. As the director had not previously said anything, I had assumed with relief that I was getting away with it, even though I knew perfectly well something was missing.

I went home and, in some panic, said to my daughter, "I don't know if I can do this! I've been acting for over forty years—how is it that I've never learned how to break down and weep on stage?!" She looked at me thoughtfully for a minute or two and then said, "Well, I don't know whether you can do it, either. But I know what you sound like when you're *really* doing it."

That is one of the most useful acting notes I have ever received. There was one more night without an audience and I had to take a huge risk. I said to the young man who was playing the sheriff, who would be on stage with me in that scene, "The end of Act II will be different tonight. I don't know what I'm going to do, but I'm going to do *something*."

All through Act I I was conscious that there was a test before me. As we moved into and through Act II the tension built inside me. I let the tension into the scene and let it build until it had to break. At that moment I changed my voice, deliberately using the sound that occurs naturally when I am overtaken by grief. It was like nothing I had ever attempted before—a completely calculated and technical approach to the moment—and it worked! The moment I changed my voice, a flood of feeling followed. I collapsed on the bench and sobbed. It was a completely real moment for me emotionally and, at the same time, I was totally aware of the progress of the end of the act. As the lights faded to black I drew the end of the last sob just into the edge of the blackout and then fell silent. We exited in the blackout. It was absolutely exhilarating, after so many years on stage, to learn something new about how to use what *is* in my own life to create what *is needed* in my character's life.

I had a further opportunity to explore the principle a few years later in an acting class I was teaching. I was directing a young woman who needed to weep in a scene and was having trouble. She was a dancer. I thought, "Well, if I could go in through my voice—which is one of my strongest areas of training—maybe as a dancer she can go in through her body." She was seated in that piece of blocking. So I suggested, "Why don't you collapse forward over your lap and let your shoulders shake." She tried it, and it helped.

I have been primarily a "Method" actor—using a subjective, feeling based approach to a part rather than an objective, technique based approach. Some actors work better from the inside out, others from the outside in. I have been an "inside-out" actor all my life, but these objective technique based lessons late in my career have been exciting and enriching.

There is an idea here that I am still exploring: as actors we not only get ourselves out of the way of the character, but we use the stuff of our own being to form the character. As followers of Christ, we find that our own difficulties turn into the very substance of our greatest ability to minister to others. In both cases, we encounter and make conscious use of our own life experiences. We make a conscious choice, as an actor, to deal truthfully with memories and/or character traits we may have preferred to ignore or gloss over in ourselves. But they are the raw stuff of which a truthful portrayal is made, and we move courageously into those places in our hearts and minds and bring from them a theatrical character. Why? Because we are called to that. Because we love God and are passionate about His hand on our lives. Our love for God and our passion for our calling cause us to create a gift. The gift is for the audience. In giving it, we pour out God's love to the audience.

The way that parallels our personal relationships is this: our time, our counsel, the giving of ourselves to a friend or child or someone whom we are mentoring—the sharing of our story and the giving of ourselves to another human—is a gift of story, just as the creation of a character for a play is a gift of story. The receiver's life is enriched because we all thirst for story. It is through story that we understand ourselves and the world around us. I think this means that the ministry that takes place through character may be similar in nature to the ministry that takes place within our own relationships.

If art can be defined as *thinking up* something beautiful and bringing it forth (and this *is* the dictionary definition), then perhaps friendship—human relationship—is meant to include *seeing* something beautiful in one another and bringing it forth. As we mature, as actors and as Christians, we undertake this work more and more selflessly, more and more unselfconsciously, and come closer to the *imago dei* we are created to be.

# THREE:
## *The Calling of Mary/Martha*

*What am I called to? As badly as I*
*want to be an actor,* **is** *there something*
*I want even more?*

*M*y current students, in their chapel services,
sing quite a bit of contemporary praise
music. Music is very active on our campus, and there
are excellent bands that form to lead the praise and
worship time in chapel. A few years ago, one of the
songs they were singing had words that say, "Lord,
I'm desperate for you; Lord, I'm lost without you."
Sometimes I could sing it. Sometimes I couldn't. It
is very important to me that I mean what I sing, just
as that I mean what I say. I found myself thinking,
"Desperate? Am I desperate? I don't think so."
Occasionally, in those days, I found myself desperate
for the Lord. Often lonely, but only occasionally

desperate. The longer I know Him, the more solid the relationship gets. In that way, He is like other friends.

It was not always so. This morning I was glancing through a nearly thirty-year- old journal, looking for a quotation that I found and will get to shortly, when I came across this entry that made me laugh aloud:

"6/17/84. Where should I go, Lord? You alone have the words of life. I tried to come to You this morning, but what is the use? Ryan is already up, throwing up and demanding cereal."

So there have been times when I felt desperate for God. I am glad that I documented some of them, since it is so easy to forget, complacently. I laughed because this same Ryan, my youngest child, is now a godly young man and a significant artist, most particularly a musician. It has been a long time since he interrupted my work by throwing up and demanding cereal. Oh, glory! At this moment I am seized with nostalgia and would gladly set aside this pad and pen to comfort a feverish, small crabby-pants. Easy to say as I gaze out wide windows at the benign, sunny prospect, squirrels racing around and pansies nodding and whispering secrets in the summer breeze.

Ryan is now the father of four and expecting a fifth child this fall. I am nearly beside myself with excitement. I suppose this child will more likely interrupt Ryan's work than mine, throwing up and demanding cereal. But, since I live in the same town, perhaps I will be blessed by that privilege once or twice.

All right. Here is the quote I was looking for. It is from Rilke's *Letters to a Young Poet:*

> You are looking outward, and that above all you should not do now. Nobody can counsel and help you, nobody. There is only one single way. Go into yourself. Search for the reason that bids you to write, find out whether it is spreading out its roots in the deepest places of your heart, acknowledge to yourself whether you would have to die if it were denied you to write. This above all—ask yourself in the stillest hour of your night: *Must* I write? Delve into yourself for a deep answer. And if this should be affirmative, if you may meet this earnest question with a strong and simple 'I must,' then build your life according to this necessity; your life even into its most indifferent and slightest hour must be a sign of this urge and testimony to it.

These words helped me very much. I was trying to balance home, family, passion for God and artistic temperament. Although I answered no to Rilke's question, I found the one to which I must answer yes, as you will presently see.

Here is a question for *you*: *Must* you act? Don't be sentimental with yourself. People in our society are drawn to the lies of acting. The lies are: you get rich; you get famous; being famous is fun; acting isn't really work; acting is easy. The facts are: acting is a great deal of work and many people give their lives to it without ever earning a living at it. If you *do* happen to get rich and famous, riches and fame have nothing to do with acting and carry their own headaches. They don't make you happy.

In our Christian culture we are taught priorities:

1. God.

2. Family.

3. Work.

It's sort of helpful if you're not ready to deal with the real list. Here's the real list:

1. God.

That's all. It feels harsh, but it is central.

It turns out we are all Mary. We are all Martha. Look:

> As Jesus and his disciples were on their way,
> he came to a village where a woman named

Martha opened her home to him. She had a sister called Mary, who sat at the Lord's feet listening to what he said. But Martha was distracted by all the preparations that had to be made. She came to him and asked, "Lord, don't you care that my sister has left me to do the work by myself? Tell her to help me!" (Luke 10:38-40)

But Jesus wouldn't do it. I suspect Martha was tired and frustrated because she, too, wanted to sit and hear the Lord. But this day she had allowed herself to become distracted, and the only way she could think of to fix things was to distract Mary, too. But neither Mary nor Jesus was buying Martha's solution.

Before God calls you to theatre he calls you to himself. Make no mistake. There is no higher call nor greater task than direct communion with God. Mary, in the above story, was powerfully drawn to that communion. We are all Mary, just as we are all Martha. As Martha we seek to serve Jesus. This is a good impulse and one that flows from our likeness to him—as servants. But we try to use our servant-hood to justify our worth. That is, we use our doing to justify our being. It doesn't. Being doesn't need justification.

When Moses said to God, "Who shall I say sent me?" God answered "I Am." Asked his identity, God affirmed his own being. Considering all the magnificent attributes of his character, isn't it somewhat amazing that the one he wanted noticed was his "Am-ness"? We are made in his image, and the same thing gives us value—our being. And in our deepest hearts, it is our being, not our doing, that cries out for recognition, for acknowledgment, for love. Just like God.

If God has called you to theatre, it isn't because his first concern is something you can do for him. There is, in fact, something you can do for him. Furthermore, you are the only one who can do it, and if you don't do it, it won't be done. But it is not central to you. Central to you—just like God—is being. Most of us have heard that "in every heart is a God shaped vacuum." I gasped in astonishment one day when I heard a speaker suggest that "in God's heart there is a you-shaped vacuum"—a Sanne-shaped vacuum in God's heart! For me it was a powerful image. If it strikes you, too, then run, do not walk, to fill that vacuum. Therein is your greatest fulfillment, your greatest joy and your greatest service.

*Secondarily*, perhaps you are an actor. If so, by all means follow your calling. It may comprise your doing, your Martha. But it can never satisfy your being, your Mary. Jesus wasn't kidding about dying in order to live. But as you lay down your life, if you are called to theatre it will not be taken from you—though you will have to give it up. It is a paradox. In some ways, John Lennon may have been right that "Life is what happens while we're making other plans." Ever since the fall of man, ever since the pure white light shivered and shattered into these extraordinary colors, we have been drawn by the colors. We cannot imagine pure white light, and we certainly cannot imagine preferring it. Wholeness surely encloses and includes brokenness. We are drawn to one color and another for personal reasons. God's purposes may be different from our own. If our being is rooted and grounded in him, our faulty perceptions don't matter. Perhaps you will star on Broadway to allow the opportunity for conversation

with the rent-a-cop at the stage door one evening—
the conversation that starts the sequence of events
that ends in the rent-a-cop's being sucked into the
rent-a-cop shaped vacuum in God's heart. So your
starring role on Broadway isn't about you at all. And
yet. And yet it is all about you because, rooted and
grounded in God, your every expression is the mirror
image of him, a mirror image possible only to you.

We tend to think that our business is to get to
Broadway while allowing God to draw us to himself.
No. Our business is to pursue God while allowing
him to get us to Broadway. Or not, as he chooses.
Our job is to die to self. Our job is to say, "Wow,
God, I love my trailer and the scene work for today
looks fabulous. Thank you. You can have it all back,
if you want." Every day.

What about success?

My friend, Joy Sawyer, has written a book of
daily devotions for artists, *The Art of the Soul:
Meditations for the Creative Spirit*. We read it in
my Introduction to Theatre classes, and the students
kept a journal in which they responded to Joy's various topics. Because Joy lives nearby, I was able to

invite her, toward the end of the semester, to come to class and meet with the students. She mediated an informal discussion on Christians in the arts, answering some questions posed by the students, asking others. A student struggling with understanding her sense of call said, "I think I am called to acting. But what if I audition and audition and audition and I'm never cast? When do I give up?" The question was earnest, intense and anguished.

Joy's response was spontaneous, sympathetic laughter filled with tender understanding out of which she said, "I don't know if you ever give up. A person called to the foreign mission field may serve for thirty years and never see a single convert. Yet, in the Christian community, we would think it presumptuous to take this situation as evidence that the person was not called." Maybe it's the same in the arts. God may have called you to audition. He may not have called you to be cast. He may have called you to theatre without calling you to visible success in theatre in the eyes of the world.

I was able to answer Rilke's question. *Must* I write? No. Very well, then—what *must* I do? And the answer came to me: "One thing I ask of the Lord, this is what I seek: that I may dwell in the house of the Lord all the days of my life, to gaze upon the beauty of the Lord and to seek him in his temple" (Psalm 27:4). *That* I *must.*

And so I did. Have. Do. You come, too.

# FOUR:
## *Gideon and Disneyland*

*Knowing God isn't part of doing theatre.*
*Doing theatre is part of knowing God.*
*How can I let Him into and through my*
*work? How can I know it's Him?*

G od does appear to call people to the acting profession. Only time and prayer can ultimately answer the question of whether you are such a person. If you are, or if you are pursuing acting while sorting out doubts about your call, you are probably considering the question of your Christian witness as it exists within your theatre life.

Witnessing is often a peculiar concept in Christian circles. As a new believer, nearly forty years ago, I was acutely aware that I had a responsibility to be witnessing to Christ. I wasn't exactly sure what that meant. I dimly thought it might have something to do with accosting strangers in their homes or at the supermarket and telling them enthusiastically about Jesus. The difficulty I experienced was that, while I certainly felt quite enthusiastic about Jesus, I didn't know him very well, or even very much about him. Normally, a witness knows something. In a court case involving an auto accident, for example, a witness is perhaps a disinterested observer who happened to see the accident and can give an authoritative, objective account to the court. As far as I have ever been able to tell, we Christians are the only group of people on earth who expect ourselves to be able to witness regarding something we haven't experienced. That can be pretty embarrassing, but it isn't fatal. We merely have the cart before the horse. The Bible actually says, "But you will receive power, *when the Holy Spirit comes on you;* and you will be my witnesses..." (Acts 1:8, italics mine).

We know that God can, and does, speak whenever, however, and through whomever he chooses— Pharaoh, Balaam's ass, and plenty of others. If you have given your life to Christ and are longing to know him and serve him, be assured your longing for him is not greater than his for you. He will not get the cart before the horse. It is extremely likely that he will speak *to* you before you will understand how, intentionally, to allow him to speak *through* you. We often say, "But how will I *know* when he speaks to me?" If you really want to know, you will learn to know.

In the following passage about Gideon's first meeting with God, we will be able to see some things God does and, perhaps, make some tentative observations about God's ways:

> The angel of the Lord came and sat down under the oak in Ophrah that belonged to Joash the Abiezrite, where his son Gideon was threshing wheat in a winepress to keep it from the Midianites. When the angel of the Lord appeared to Gideon, he said, "The Lord is with you, mighty warrior." "But sir," Gideon replied, "if the Lord is with us, why has all this happened to us? Where are all his wonders that our fathers told us about when they said, 'Did not the Lord bring us up out of Egypt?' But now the Lord has abandoned us and put us into the hand of Midian."

> The Lord turned to him and said, "Go in the strength you have and save Israel out of Midian's hand. Am I not sending you?"

> "But Lord," Gideon asked, "how can I save Israel? My clan is the weakest in Manasseh, and I am the least in my family."

The Lord answered, "I will be with you, and you will strike down all the Midianites together."

Gideon replied, "If now I have found favor in your eyes, give me a sign that it is really you talking to me. Please do not go away until I come back and bring my offering and set it before you."

Gideon went in, prepared a young goat, and from an ephah of flour he made bread without yeast. Putting the meat in a basket and its broth in a pot, he brought them out and offered them to him under the oak.

The angel of God said to him, "Take the meat and the unleavened bread, place them on this rock, and pour out the broth." And Gideon did so. With the tip of the staff that was in his hand, the angel of the Lord touched the meat and the unleavened bread. Fire flared from the rock, consuming the meat and the bread. And the angel of the Lord disappeared. When Gideon realized that it was the angel of the Lord, he exclaimed, "Ah, Sovereign Lord! I have seen the angel of the Lord face to face!" (Judges 6:11-22).

In this short passage a number of things are worth looking at. First of all, let us observe the circumstances of Gideon at the time the angel of the Lord appears. The first ten verses of Judges 6 tell us that the Israelites had fallen away from the Lord and he had given them into the hand of the Midianites for seven years, until things got so bad that the Israelites cried out to God. Although it is not immediately apparent to Gideon, the angel of the Lord appears to him as an answer to the prayers of the Israelites.

Where does the angel of the Lord find Gideon? Threshing wheat in a wine press. Threshing wheat involves throwing it in the air so the wind can bear away the dust and chaff while the heavier grain falls to the ground. It is meant to be done on a large, sometimes outdoor, threshing floor where the wind can move freely, separating the grain from the chaff. To undertake this task in a secret, enclosed space, hoping not to be noticed by the Midianites, would be hot, sweaty, chokingly dirty work—not to mention the fear of discovery. Gideon is in this situation because the Midianites have been allowed to overrun the Israelites, leaving them destitute. If they find Gideon with grain, they will take it, perhaps leaving his family to starve. This is the moment God has chosen to intervene. The angel of the Lord's opening remark would certainly be downright infuriating. I doubt Gideon is feeling much like a mighty warrior. He asks several short tempered questions, which the angel of the Lord ignores, giving him, instead, a commission.

To this, Gideon replies, more or less, "You've got the wrong guy." By now, however, something about the angel of the Lord has captured Gideon's attention and quickened his hope. He asks for a sign. He asks for time to prepare a gift. The angel of the Lord agrees to wait. It only takes a few seconds to read the next few lines, but look at what Gideon does. In a society with no refrigeration, no electricity, no running water or gas stove, he catches and slaughters a kid—a lamb or baby goat—preparing it for a meal; and he makes unleavened cakes (he bakes bread). He brings this cooked food to the angel of the Lord—how many hours later? The angel of the Lord, true to his word, is still there. Not only that, but his next actions implicitly acknowledge the magnitude of Gideon's gift.

You remember we discovered Gideon threshing wheat in a wine press—wheat that was desperately needed by his family in a starving and oppressed economy. Yet he baked bread. He also killed a kid. That kid, grown, would have provided twice the meat. If it was a doe, it might have provided another kid, milk and cheese, as well. The angel of the Lord honored Gideon by accepting the gift in its entirety. He let Gideon cook all day, then he didn't even feed him. Instead, he accepted the gift in a manner that clearly revealed and confirmed his identity to Gideon: "Then Gideon perceived that it was the angel of Yahweh." Gideon got everything he needed from the encounter. He may have gone to bed physically hungry that night, but he knew who he had been talking with, and he remembered that the angel of the Lord had called him a mighty warrior. That personal encounter fortified him for the dialogue surrounding the fleece, for the stripping away of the vast majority of his troops, for the encounter with the enemy and for victory. The encounter at the oak tree began the process of making Gideon a witness. You can read Gideon's entire story in Judges 6-9 in the Old Testament.

God speaks through the Bible as we read it. He also speaks through circumstances, but we have to be careful about drawing conclusions too soon. Things didn't look too good for Christianity after the crucifixion and before the resurrection. God also speaks through other believers and through our prayer times. The more time we make for Him in prayer, the more He may say. It helps sometimes to sit in silence, not considering the conversation over just because we have said all we have to say. Wait to hear what He has to say. You will not know His voice immediately and with certainty, but you will grow more sure over time.

In the early weeks of 1983 I asked the Lord if we could take the children to Disneyland at Christmas. "We've never had a proper family vacation," I said, "and it would be so much fun for them."

"No," he said.

That was all.

No.

I was embarrassed and my feelings were hurt, but I dropped the subject. A few days later he reintroduced it. "Actually," he said, "I'd like for you to go in June." I was overjoyed.

"What do you think?" I asked my husband, Tom.

"I don't know. He hasn't said anything to me."

"Yes, well, I can see that might be a problem. On the other hand, he almost never talks to you this way, and he often does to me, so how about if you request your vacation time for the last two weeks of June and we'll see what happens?"

That seemed good to Tom, and so he made the arrangement. Now, understand, our annual income in these years was habitually somewhere near the national poverty line—give or take a few hundred bucks from year to year. So trusting God for a trip to Disneyland for the five of us was certainly an exercise in listening. Except we sort of stopped listening. Without ever getting what felt like concrete evidence, we began to behave as though we were definitely going. We told the children. We made arrangements to meet Tom's parents there, about a 10 hour drive for them. The only trouble was, we were still unable, from paycheck to paycheck, to set aside anything for the trip. The weeks of spring sped by and quite quickly June 15th rolled around. Tom was the overnight disc jockey for a local Christian radio station. He came home at seven in the morning on the 15$^{th}$ and we looked at one another bleakly. We were scheduled to leave for California the morning of the 16$^{th}$. The children were counting on it. Tom's parents were counting on it. And we didn't have one nickel towards the trip.

"I guess we blew it," Tom said, gallantly sharing the blame. "But everybody is looking forward to it so much, we can't disappoint them. We're going to have to pull it off somehow," we decided. So we jumped in the car and drove around to banks and lenders. But nobody would lend to us. We arrived home around eleven a.m. Tom was white with exhaustion.

"Look," I said, "you haven't even been to bed yet, and you have to work again tonight. Why don't you go get some sleep and I'll sit down on the couch and try to have this out with God." So Tom went to bed and I went to the living room.

"I don't understand," I said. "When I first asked and you said no, I accepted that. You're the one who came back with the counter offer. I've asked and asked since then to know the truth, not to be deceived. I have been so happy to think you were doing this for us, but if you are not, all you had to do was say so. I feel embarrassed and ashamed, and I can't stand it that the kids have to have this huge disappointment, and what are Tom's parents going to say?"

I was pretty worked up. I was crying. God wasn't upset. He spoke calmly.

"You know Abraham?" he asked.

"Yes," I blubbered.

"You know Jesus?"

"Yes."

"Well, I asked Abraham for something one time, and when it came time, he didn't actually have to do it. I asked Jesus for something one time, too. When it came time, he actually had to go through with it."

"I'm going to ask you for something right now, and I'm not going to tell you whether this is an Abraham situation or a Jesus situation."

There was a short pause. Then he said, "I want you to give me back the trip."

I thought for a long time. This was difficult. Not so much losing the trip—though I was keenly aware of the disappointment the children would feel. But this: the trip had as yet no substance on the physical plane. If I gave it back and he took it, the only evidence I would have of the transaction would be our highly abstract and ephemeral conversations on the subject. In short, I might never know for sure whether God had spoken or the whole thing had taken place in my fantasies.

I wrestled.

Finally, "all right," I said. Tom had to work one more overnight shift before the start of vacation. I decided we would all go with him. The kids enjoyed the big, empty station at night and sometimes, for a special treat, he let them say something on the air at 3:30 or 4 in the morning. I thought it would be good for us all to be together in the final hours of the test, to have the joy or the disappointment together.

When I was all done, and the transaction was completed, I said, "One more thing. If all this has been for me, and the rest of the family doesn't have to go through it, I want you to stop it now, before I have to tell Tom."

As I said the word "now", the telephone rang. No foolin'. Right on the word. It was our pastor's wife.

She said, "Listen. I have some money we've been meaning to give you for your trip, only I haven't gotten around to getting it to you. Are you going to be home? Can I swing by?" She brought us $364. All day the phone and doorbell rang with more gifts. Also, we received a check we were expecting from work, but it was substantially more than we had anticipated.

We didn't need to go to the radio station with Tom that night. We needed to pack. The next morning we drove away to California in our van with our three children and $1,600 in cash for the trip. That was thirty years ago, and the trip remains for me one of those incandescent family vacation memories which only grow more golden with the passage of time. God did promise me Disneyland. And he delivered. I witnessed it.

Looking back these years later, I see that God was working strongly in my life at that period through story. He was speaking *to* me in *my* story in preparation to speak *through* me, both through my own story and then through others.

In my life God has used Bible reading, Bible meditation, Bible study, Godly counsel, prayer and time. This is not the place for a detailed discussion of all these avenues, but you should pursue them individually, some simultaneously and some at other times.

# FIVE:
## Children and Windows

*Why did Jesus instruct us to be like little children?*

Jesus took a small child and, placing her in their midst, he said, "Unless you become like this, you will never enter the kingdom of heaven."

It is often remarked that actors—artists in general—never grow up. This idea is used to excuse and explain irresponsibility and immorality on the part of the actors and to excuse and explain why the rest of us aren't artists. We feel simultaneously beyond such childish things and totally inadequate to attain to such heights. We feel hero worship and condescension. Notice I say we. I am an artist. There is a good chance, if you are reading this, that you are an artist or hope and long to be one. But, tucked away inside every artist is a non-artist—judging, editing, often condemning the artist and the art.

Only very small children have no opinion as to whether they, themselves, are artists. They paint, draw, sing, act, dance and build. But they don't think of themselves as artists. They know they are little children. In grownup terms they aren't anything yet. And we know that we are children of God, but it is yet to be seen what we shall be—except we know that when we see him we shall be like him. Well—in heaven, of course. But what about in the meantime? Is it possible that *every* time we see him we are just like him?

There are lessons for us here as actors. One of the lessons is guilelessness—transparency. For years, as a young Christian, I heard that we are supposed to be transparent. This means, of course, that you should be able to see right through me—an expression by which we mean that you would know all about me. But one day I was looking through a beautifully clean window at a lovely hillside with blue sky and clouds. I knew I was inside a house. I appreciatively noticed how clean the window was, but mostly I looked at the hill and the sky and the clouds. The cleanness of the window didn't cause me to contemplate the window. Instead, it invited my attention to something further away, something *else* on the *other side* of the window—something I could never have noticed at all if there had been a wall there instead of a window. My transparency, then, doesn't invite your attention to me. It invites your attention to Christ. My transparency as an actor is a window through which others may see God's truth through story—one of His most appealing, and apparently one of His favorite, forms for revealing truth.

Some time ago my friend and I toured, off and on for several years, a production that chronicled the life of Abraham and Sarah. It was a little over an hour long, written in contemporary, poetic language. We ran it for a short time in our own theatre and then made it available for tour. It was popular. Long after we had "closed" it and gone on to other projects, groups would request it. Since it involved only the two of us, we would occasionally pull it together again and do another performance or two for various groups. The long, leisurely and interrupted production process allowed us to continue learning about these two Biblical characters. In rehearsals I said, "Lord, I didn't know Sarah. But You did. Will You put something true in my portrayal of her?" I believe He did. It may not have been factual, but it was true.

One of my favorite discoveries was that Sarah—at least *this* Sarah, in this production of this script—this Sarah was highly amused when Abraham told her about God's plan that he be circumcised. Imagine! These are desert nomads. Nobody has ever done such a thing before. Not only is he being circumcised, and imposing it on his 13-year-old son, but he has to have all his male servants circumcised, too! What a mutiny that could have caused! But God was in it—so they all agreed. Meanwhile, Sarah, in the indulgent way of women everywhere towards their men's outlandish ideas—Sarah was giggling uncontrollably with her eyes lowered and her hand covering her mouth!

Scripture doesn't tell us what Sarah thought of the circumcision. There is a certain dramatic license in deciding what is appropriate to a character. But the storytelling license of theatre brought Abraham and Sarah to life in ways that encouraged and uplifted people and brought them close to God's personal storybook in new ways. All true stories have the potential to bring us close to God—whether or not the true stories are factual.

One day I was teaching a creative drama class with a group of 4-year-olds. Who else enters into story with such unapologetic enthusiasm? We were working with the Bible story of the woman who loses a coin and sweeps the whole place diligently looking for it. I had brought in a large cardboard box full of crumpled newspapers with a penny in the bottom. I had them open the box, look through the papers and find the penny. Then I told them the story (Luke 15:8ff). I had them act it out in small groups, praising their work. After one or two groups had gone, instead of taking the story for their source, the next groups began to imitate each other's actions, doing what those just ahead of them had done—probably because I had praised that work and they therefore concluded that their playmates were "doing it right." But, of course, they lost the freshness of the actual task. In an attempt to draw them back, I said, "O.k., wonderful! You're doing great! This time I want you to try something a little different. Instead of pretending that you're looking for a coin, I want you to pretend that you're *really* looking for a coin." They immediately grasped the distinction, and their next playings of the scene were captivatingly fresh and truthful.

There was a story of Sir Tyrone Guthrie that made the rounds during the early days of the Guthrie Theatre in Minneapolis. Purportedly, Sir Tyrone would appear on stage in the middle of crowd scenes in rehearsal, threading his way among the crowds and murmuring with breathless interest to various individual crowd members, "And what are *you* pretending to do?" I had that story from a member of the Guthrie acting company with whom I was friends in those days. I have later concluded that, as actors, *whatever* we are "pretending to do," we must always find a way to pretend that we are *really* doing it!

We are seeking truth in our actions onstage. This intention can lead to some interesting discussions with ourselves about the characters we are playing. Two particular scenarios come to mind. The first is villainous.

Villains are bad guys and we have known since childhood that they are—how shall I say it—WRONG! The interesting and necessary awareness for an actor to have is that no one is wrong *in his own eyes*. That is, everyone has a "good" reason for everything they do, a reason that justifies the action in their eyes. From Hitler's point of view, ethnic cleansing was a good idea. It would rid the world of undesirable elements and leave a strong, healthy, beautiful Master Race. From the perspective of Pontius Pilate, he was dealing with a people's holiday and a tradition attached to it. He saw no fault in Jesus, but the people wanted Barabbas released instead, so he indulged the people. It seemed to him the best idea at the time. Probably neither Hitler nor Pilate was familiar with the scriptural warning, "There is a way that seems right to a man, but in the end it leads to death" (Proverbs 14:12).

Most, if not all, evil is rooted in fear. If we can identify a character's fear—even one not acknowledged by the character—it can take us a long way towards finding his motivations, his reasons, his self-justification, his version of truth.

The other area I wish to discuss of truth in character has to do with romantic relationships on stage. We know that other artists have various media with which to work—paint, canvas, clay, musical instruments, and so forth. As actors, we have ourselves, our bodies and voices. We are the medium of our art. In addition to bodies and voices, our emotions are also part of our stock in trade. It is extremely easy to deceive oneself into believing that a character's romantic attraction to another character is "real." I perceive it as "my" attraction to the person opposite whom I am playing. I think this deception works great harm in Hollywood and elsewhere.

The attractions may be to any other member of the company, and are not always heterosexual.

Working together creatively invites intimacy, and living in Western culture today promotes physical intimacy.

Homosexuality is a difficult topic because emotional stakes are so high. If I perceive something as internal to my nature—"the way I am"—then I may become very afraid to consider that being this way is not "all right."

The Bible is brief in its remarks about homosexuality. It is downright chatty on the subject of money. Yet the Christian church sometimes seems far more tolerant of financial crimes than of homosexuality. Why is that, I wonder?

Working in theatre one encounters open, flamboyant homosexuality—perhaps one sees it more there than in other lines of work. The Christian church is divided on the subject. God is not. Thankfully, He has promised that if we seek Him we will find Him. Jeremiah 31:33-34 makes a tremendous promise:

> 'This is the covenant I will make with the house of Israel after that time," declares the Lord. "I will put my law in their minds and write it on their hearts. I will be their God, and they will be my people. No longer will a

man teach his neighbor, or a man his brother, saying, 'Know the Lord,' because they will all know me, from the least of them to the greatest," declares the Lord. "For I will forgive their wickedness and will remember their sins no more."

This is an Old Testament promise about the New Testament covenant. It refers to the indwelling of the Holy Spirit within the believer.

To balance so great a freedom, we are cautioned to meet together prayerfully. Hebrews 10:25 admonishes us: "Let us not give up meeting together, as some are in the habit of doing, but let us encourage one another—and all the more as you see the Day approaching." It is easy to allow ourselves to be driven from believing fellowship by our own fears and doubts. It is uncomfortable to hold a minority view on any subject. But God is never offended by our real and urgent questions, and He holds final authority.

One of my most precious and comforting memories is of an exchange I heard between my husband and an older, more mature believer many years ago. Shortly after he began to follow Christ, my husband remarked, "I guess I'll have to quit smoking dope, huh?" Our friend replied, "Wow. I don't know. I wouldn't worry about it. The Holy Spirit will let you know." My heart longs for more such conversations. If we all extended that grace to one another on a regular basis, perhaps people really *would* know we are Christians by our love.

Through diligent and prayerful study and discussion of the Word, we must come to some discernment *within our believing communities* as to what the Bible says about the sinfulness of homosexuality. If the community with whom we meet determines it to be sin, we might do well to consider that it may be, at least some of the time, a sin based on a misunderstanding of the nature of love. Homophobia, on the other hand, is based entirely on hate and fear, and there is no room for it in a Christian's heart or mind.

I counsel my actors to assume that any romantic attachment that arises during work on a show is a product of that work. I strongly advise them not to talk about it even with each other until six weeks after the show closes. We are instructed, "Above all

else, guard your heart, for it is the wellspring of life"
(Proverbs 4:23). If we are serious about pursuing
Christ, we must do this—we must guard our hearts.
If the attachment is more than artistic, and if it is of
the Lord, it will keep.

# SIX:
## *Story and Message*

*Looking for the truth in the story is a good way to see whether a project is worthy of you—your time, your energy, your presence, your—well, your likeness to God.*

There is a way in which artistic transparency parallels spiritual transparency. If my being spiritually transparent causes you to see not me but Christ through me, is it possible that my artistic transparency can have a similar effect? If I am doing my job on stage, the audience is able to encounter the story in a meaningful way. Just like listening to Jesus tell parables, we should be able, as audience, to connect the story to *our* story and to connect both to The Story. That's a key way we learn. Jesus said he taught in parables because most peoples' minds weren't wired to accept straight information. We're inclined to think of that as a fault, but maybe it's just a human characteristic. The human spirit is like a heat seeking missile—except it seeks truth. It will find and cling to whatever truth it is capable of recognizing in whatever story it encounters.

Young Christian actors are often troubled by questions like, "Should I kiss someone on stage?" "Should I play a prostitute, or an embezzler?" These questions cannot be answered because their focus is insufficient. The answer may change with circumstances. Should I play a thief or a prostitute? A thief crucified with Jesus or Mary Magdalene in a passion play? Probably. The Bible is full of kissing and of people whose morals are questionable. These people aren't always the bad guys. Jacob. Rahab. David and Bathsheba. A better question might be, "What is the story saying?" Francis Schaeffer discusses the idea that art has major and minor themes. In Christian art, he says, the major theme is redemption. The minor theme is fallenness. Surely the purpose in portraying fallenness would be related somehow to redemption. That seems to be the overall basis for God's choice of stories, and we might do well to consider it as wisely as we can in our own choices. There are certainly individual stories in the Bible wherein we cannot readily discern the relationship of the story and/or the characters to redemption. That's all right. God can. The connections in our own choices may not be immediately apparent to every believer, either, but they must be apparent to us. There should be a perceptible (to us) path to Christ through every role, every production we undertake. There is no art for art's sake in the Christian life. There is no *anything* for its own sake. *Everything* is for Christ's sake.

The arts, like everything else since the Fall, are seriously awry. When our spirits are drawn to the arts by God, our flesh is very likely to become noisy and overly excited. Performance arts, in particular, in our society are highly self-centric. Flesh-self. How you look, how you speak, how you sing, how you dance, your hair color, muscle tone and physical charisma are deeply important to auditions. Unusual skill and talent, plus rigorous training, might get you the audition. A quarter inch of extra or missing height might get you cut. So, naturally, we become rather preoccupied with the flesh.

I appreciate David Mamet's reminder that personal character is the most relevant and interesting character we can ever bring on stage. For a Christian, the development of personal character is about dying to self and living to Christ—"I no longer live but Christ lives in me." Is it possible that my transparency on stage in a role—say, Blanche du Bois from *A Streetcar Named Desire*—can invite audience attention to something further away, something *else* on the *other side* of the window—something they could never have noticed at all if I had been a wall instead of a window? May my transparency—on stage as well as in real life—invite attention not to me but to Christ? I believe so. I believe that to watch Blanche du Bois in all her courage, hope, vanity and failure can create such a cry in the human heart that it breaks into colored shards of compassion and longing and sends forth its search for truth with renewed determination. We don't need to always be passing out answers. Sometimes, we only need to be creating hunger. If people can be brought to seek, they will find. It is promised.

Jesus went about doing good. He fed and healed people and he told stories. The stories also fed and healed people, as well as creating hunger. As actors, we are called to the same work. It is interesting to me that Jesus seldom gave a straight answer to a question. Instead, he countered with another question. Observation suggests that people are most deeply content with answers they figure out for themselves. A line may be the shortest distance between two points, but it is not always the most satisfactory.

When my son, Ryan, was four or five, one day he was troubled. He was the youngest of my three children. He asked me, "Why don't I understand multiplication? Sasha and Colin do." I suppose I could have said, "You're too little." I was also the youngest of three and goodness knows I had heard that often enough. Instead, I asked, "Do you remember when you were little and couldn't reach the light switch?" He nodded. "And then you got bigger and you could?" He nodded again. "You didn't have to do anything on purpose to make that happen, did you?" He shook his head. "Your body just grew," I said. "That's what it does. That's what your mind does, too. When it is time for you to understand multiplication, you will." He went away perfectly satisfied—for the moment, at least. Because I took time to find an analogy in his life that he was already familiar with, he could follow the new ideas, too.

Jesus used that method sometimes. In answer to the question, "Who is my neighbor?" he spun an engaging prime time TV story with which his audience could all identify. People were always getting mugged on the Jericho Road. It was a serious problem!

Jesus always knew what question he was answering and who in the audience was having that question. As actors, we are not in charge of which questions show up in the text of a given play. But we know what the major life questions are. They are the same questions we have, or have had. Like Jesus, as playwrights and as actors, we can cultivate the habit of helping people find answers for themselves. This is a delicate under-taking. Much of what is called "church drama" falls flat because it is tediously didactic—it bops people over the head with answers. There is no mystery. Bertolt Brecht got run out of his country partly because his theatre stirred people's active interest in the Marxist Revolution. It has been centuries since Christian actors got regularly run out of town because their performances stirred active interest in the living God.

I am not suggesting that it is even possible—let alone expected—for one actor in one show to singlehandedly change the direction of public opinion regarding Jesus Christ. I *am* suggesting that an individual performer should be aware of whose troops she is reinforcing in the spiritual battle. I ask myself: What is this play saying? Is its major theme fallenness or redemption? If the play or role seems swallowed by fallenness, is it showing something we need to know about fallenness in order to create a longing for redemption? What must I do with my body and voice to portray this character? Can I do these things and honor Christ?

There is no one set of rules. Everything depends on your relationship with Christ. Rules actually make it possible not to listen to Christ. With rules we think we already have the correct answers.

When I was about nineteen years old, my theatre history professor remarked one day that the quality of our lives is determined in large part by our tolerance for ambiguity. I never forgot she said those words, and it has been interesting to watch that thought weave through various phases of my life.

On the whole, principles are more useful than rules. "Never go barefoot on stage" is a useful rule while you are building the set. It becomes a serious hindrance during performances of *Huckleberry Finn!* Principles are ideas like, "Honor God. Consider others better than yourself. Love your colleagues. Don't be ashamed of the gospel." These ideas translate between circumstances. If we pursue Christ fully as we pursue acting, it is likely we will find ways to feed and heal both our co-workers and our audiences, over time, with the fruit of our own stories and of the stories we choose to act.

Kierkegaard said that product comes unswervingly from process. Jesus said a tree is known by its fruit.

# SEVEN:
## *Actions and Words*

*What is acting? Acting is doing. As*
*Christians, to what do we want to give*
*the power of our doing?*

$\mathscr{I}$ have believed for years that if I so much
as wave my arm through the air, the ripple
effect of that motion will reach the farthest star.

Madeleine L'Engle, again in *Walking on Water,*
speaks of astronauts in space hearing a radio program that had been broadcast in the 1930s. No one
was playing it. It was just—there.

Scripture tells us that what has been whispered
in secret will be shouted from the rooftops, and
that we will be held accountable for every word we
utter. We have heard these things, of course, yet in
the face of this solemn acknowledgment of words,
we stoutly assert that "actions speak louder."

In theatre we are deliberate about the relation-ship between actions and words, carefully crafting their intersections to form what we hope will be meanings—meanings received as we have meant them by audience/spectators. Perhaps Jesus told stories as a kind of back door entrance into the consciousness of his hearers. In the movie, *My Big Fat Greek Wedding*, the heroine wants her father to do something. "Let me talk to him," cautions her mother, "he has to think it's his idea." Again, in the movie about the Beach Boys' life, they want Murray Wilson to do something, but someone points out, "he has to think it's his idea."

Are we all infected with this virus? I think so, to some extent. In western society, at least, the prefer-ence for drawing our own conclusions shows up by about eighteen months of age, and never completely disappears, so it is either inherent or very effectively taught—and very thoroughly learned.

Jesus, who alone on the planet had the right to be utterly didactic, chose not to be so. Much that is wrong with "Christian" theatre—or Marxist theatre or any other agenda laden theatre—could be remedied if we would remember that didacticism is not our place. What do we want to say? If some radio program broadcast *once* seventy plus years ago is still floating around, what about *The Sound of Music?* What about the Latin Mass? Within this understanding of the power and permanence of words, to what words do I want to give my voice? My actions?

What is acting, anyway? Two terms from long past come to me. We used them interchangeably in childhood, but now I want to use them to make a distinction. (We were able to use them interchangeably as children, I think, because the distinction I am about to draw becomes apparent only as we become adult.) The terms are "pretend" and "make believe." Sir Tyrone Guthrie, I believe, was addressing—in his wandering on stage among crowd scenes—the meaning of "pretend" that I want to unfold. It is the meaning we find in "pretender to the throne"—that is, someone all dressed up in a fiction about being the king when everybody, including himself, knows he isn't. There is a lot of that sort of thing going on in theatre today. But the real goods—what we actually go to the theatre for (and it can exist in the most spotty and inconstant fashion in the midst of pretense)—is make believe. To make believe is perhaps the closest we come, as humans, to *ex nihilo* creation. That is because, in material terms, belief is made from nothing. The thing that keeps belief from being true *ex nihilo* creation is that belief, in absolutely full flower, continues to be incorporeal. *Ex nihilo* creation results in stuff—stuff like dirt and water and the pen with which I am writing on the yellow lined pad that becomes the book you are holding. Belief, while equally weighty, weighs on a different scale. Belief is an idea—an idea to which I have committed the weight of my being. Beliefs, like ideas, matter. They take on matter—they work out in the flesh.

Finishing my undergraduate degree—which I did in my forties—I was sitting in a World History class one day when the professor, in the middle of a lecture, remarked, "Ideas matter." I suppose he went on to say other things, but I was transported by that thought for the remainder of the session. Madeleine L'Engle's book, *A Wind in the Door,* contains a passage in which Meg, a teenage girl, addresses a large and very imposing angelic being—by which she feels intimidated—by asking if he can't somehow look different. The angelic being somewhat indignantly states that he cannot do that. He can become invisible if necessary, but "when I take on matter, this is what I look like." To matter. To take on matter. Ideas matter. But they aren't flesh. And "believe," if you will, is even less flesh than "belief." Belief, after all, is a noun. What is a noun? In elementary school they taught us that a noun is the name of a person, place or thing—by saying "belief," we attribute thingness. But the expression in question isn't "make belief." It is "make believe." How wise we are when we aren't even looking! "Believe" is a verb—an action word. It isn't something that *is;* it's something that we *do*. It only exists in the moment of doing, like theatre. But it exists as truth, again like theatre—or at least like theatre is meant to be.

The relationship between pretend and make believe may be likened to the relationship between wheat and weeds spoken of by Jesus in Matthew 13:24-30:

> He set another parable before them, saying, "The Kingdom of Heaven is like a man who sowed good seed in his field, but while people

slept, his enemy came and sowed darnel weeds also among the wheat, and went away. But when the blades sprang up and brought forth fruit, then the darnel weeds appeared also. The servants of the householder came and said to him, 'Sir, didn't you sow good seed in your field? Where, then, did this darnel come from?' "He said to them, 'An enemy has done this.' "The servants asked him, 'Do you want us to go and gather them up?' "But he said, 'No, lest perhaps while you gather up the darnel weeds, you root up the wheat with them. Let both grow together until the harvest, and in the harvest time I will tell the reapers, "First, gather up the darnel weeds and bind them in bundles to burn them; but gather the wheat into my barn.""" (World English Bible)

I once heard a teaching on this passage which suggested that darnel is a weed which closely resembles wheat, and that it is impossible to tell them apart until maturity. At maturity, the heads of the wheat produce kernels of wheat, while the darnel remains empty husks. If that is the case, pretend resembles make believe in much the same way. Fully formed, they may have identical external characteristics. But what is missing from pretense and present in make believe is the very heart of the matter, the life giving property—the truth.

Everyone is born with the ability to make believe. Very early we learn from one another and from the Father of Lies how to pretend. Adults who function as artists continue to make believe. Those actors who perform the truth on stage before us, in fiction or fact, are making believe. These are the actors we long to see, and these are the performances that thrill, and do not disappoint, our souls. Those actors who are not making believe are merely pretending. No matter how skillful and well intentioned, they are missing the fat of the feast for themselves, and they are robbing their audience.

A terrible reality of our culture today is that we have all become so adept at pretense and so accustomed to it that we offer our highest honors to excellent pretense, recognizing its many merits and thinking the fault is ours if we come away still hungry. Some of the big Broadway touring shows are a part of this confusion. It *is* breathtaking to see some of the costumes, sets and lighting effects that modern technology has made possible. It *is* thrilling to see a helicopter land on stage. Thrilling and distracting. Often, sadly, we don't any longer even recognize the hunger. Instead, we deny it. How dare I think anything could possibly be missing when there is a waterfall...a swimming pool...a running river right there on stage? What *could* be missing? It must be my fault if I didn't "get it." Still, in the midst of this state of affairs, there comes to us occasionally a live performance that truly captivates us, beyond our expectation or even our ability to articulate the experience. These actors are making believe.

Strangely, these actors are often underpaid professionals in little known companies—or amateurs. Bertolt Brecht has a couple of essays in which he contrasts professional with non-professional theatre. Non-professionals come to rehearsal from a hard day's work. They struggle to find time and energy for their art, and their struggle is perceptible in their work. But they also have passion and that, too, is perceptible in their work. Brecht remarks that an actor who is paid a living wage and spared the suffering conflicts of his non-professional brother often responds by losing his passion. It is true. We've all seen perfunctory professional performances and passionate amateur performances. It is puzzling. Is it possible that, when we no longer have to lay our supper on the line—or a decent night's sleep—it somehow becomes easier to forget to lay our souls on the line? Laying our souls on the line—our hearts, our minds, our willingness to go where the script takes us in truth—is the very core of make believe.

I hope Mrs. Watts in *A Trip to Bountiful* was an example of this make believe. I got there through pretense—through the deliberate mechanism of starting to cry for no reason in Sanne's life. Each night, as I did that, I found Mrs. Watts' grief. There is a cost to expressing grief, even fictional grief. But the joy of make believe far outweighs the cost.

While we are meditating on the meaning of words, what about "actor"? What a name! To act, in the ordinary, daily sense, is to *do* something. To take action is a deliberate, energetic response to a stimulus, often with the intention to bring change or affirmation. Is acting—in the sense of making believe—also this? Most of us involved in acting would say yes. At least a qualified yes. Maybe, even, acting on stage doubles the stakes of acting off stage. On stage, in making believe, or even in pretending, the character's action is a deliberate, energetic response to a stimulus. This response creates the line, that is the direction, of the performance. *Simultaneously*, there is a *reason* for the play or performance, and that *reason* may mean the play or performance is a deliberate, energetic response to a stimulus—social, political, philosophical, religious. The craft of acting requires the blending of these two agendas in an artistic way.

As a Christian artist, I want to do my work within yet a third circle, and that circle would be the conscious reflection of the image of God. Upon further thought, I don't believe I agree with Camus' alleged statement (quoted earlier) that "if the world were clear there would be no art." I believe the world will, one day, be clear. And I believe there will still be art, because I believe artistry is human creativity at work reflecting an image of God that is not reflected in any other human work.

The Bible tells us the story of Jesus, and his story is clean and pure—no sin. Even when he was cursing the fig tree, whipping the money changers out of the temple, asking his father in Gethsemane if there was some way out of the crucifixion, there was no sin. The Bible has other stories, too—lots of them—cataloging most sins and implying the rest. Jesus even told some of those stories.

I tell stories, too. Two of my early memories illustrate a relationship between story and Story— mine and His. The first of these two memories is, in fact, my earliest memory, and it is of the day of my third birthday party. On this day, I had an encounter with my father that caused me great harm. Nearly the next thing I remember is at the age of six, when I had the great joy of being in a play at school. I was dressed in a lovely, soft, brown leather garment with a fringed hem. (Something whispers to me that it may have been a paper grocery sack, but even my senses witness to the leather—a possibly profound tribute to the truthfulness of child's play.) I was portraying a Native American mother and I knelt, down left on the stage, singing a lullaby to the baby in my arms.

The fact that my earliest memory is of harm and my next memory is of make believe suggests to me that somewhere between the ages of three and six I found that my own story was not a safe one and sought refuge in other stories. I lived most of my childhood immersed in children's fiction. I actually forgot all about that school play until one night when I was twenty-seven. I was sitting in a rocking chair cuddling my own first child in the middle of the night with moonlight pouring in the window. She was only a few days old and, as I gazed into her eyes, marveling at the miracle of her existence, the memory of my school play when I was six sprang suddenly into my mind. I was amazed to realize that I had felt exactly the same way acting the part of a mother when I was six as I now felt actually holding my own beautiful baby. This knowledge has powerfully influenced my work with child actors. I understood in that moment—and have confirmed since—that children have all the depths of emotional sensibilities that adults have. All they lack—when they lack anything—is the vocabulary to describe those depths. Directors who work well with children are successful at helping them find the vocabulary.

Now that I am a grown woman who has experienced considerable emotional healing, I have reconnected with my own story. I look back and I am grateful, awed and curious at the role other stories played in my survival and healing. I would venture to say that story is an essential component of healthy human growth. We are meant to be deeply engaged with our own stories, but when circumstances make that difficult, we can survive on other stories. The stories need to be truthful—not necessarily factual, but truthful—in order to be food for the wounded spirit. And all our spirits are wounded. The pursuit of science and the pursuit of fiction are two ways we seek to dress the wounds. Science seeks truth through fact. Fiction, perhaps, seeks a distillation of truth in which fact becomes less central, more hypothetical. The ability to perceive fact and truth as separate is a little like the ability to see color— which you will remember is a product of fractured light. Story is one of the great healing salves for brokenness in humans. We grow so accustomed to picking our way through the fallen world that we forget it is fallen. We forget *we* are fallen and are repeatedly startled when ragged chunks of life keep breaking off in our hands. Perhaps the task of the storyteller—of the actor—is to catch the falling chunks and restore them to order. This cannot be done scientifically. It must be done mythically— through story. It is deeply moving to me that God himself invents and invests in story and Story.

I used to be worried about myths. Creation myths. Resurrection myths. Osiris and so forth. If these various people groups were only dimly connected to certain principles of truth in creating their myths, I mused, who was to say we Christians weren't in the same boat, trying to come up with a whole story based on fragments of information? As I grew in my faith and understanding, I set aside that fear and began to see that in Jesus Christ fact and truth meet perfectly. God's Story, expressed through the perfect Word, Jesus Christ, is perfect Fact and perfect Truth. And what did Jesus do? He fed people, he forgave people, he healed people, and he told stories!

We tell our children stories to soothe and calm them, to instruct them, to enrich them and to delight them. If we are invited into the Kingdom only as we become as children, may we not believe our Father tells us stories for the same reasons?

I read to my children for years. They were spread over eleven years, so it always seemed natural to keep reading stories—the older ones nostalgically enjoyed the earlier books, and the youngest got to hear some terrific books way before he would have been ready to read them on his own. The part that absolutely enchanted me was that, eventually, they began reading aloud to me—books they had discovered that I didn't know about. I had read to them for so long that we stopped perceiving it as "something you do with children" and began perceiving it as "something people do together."

Theatre, as I have mentioned, is storytelling. If storytelling is "something people do together" and if Jesus walked around the countryside telling stories, there is no reason for Christians to feel apologetic about being involved in theatre—and every reason to believe God has, indeed, called us to it. Like any other honorable work, there are godly ways to pursue it and ungodly ways—and they aren't all as plain as the nose on your face. Because it is difficult to be truly and persistently Christian in the modern, generally relativistic world, we sometimes become rather dogmatic about certain matters that could just as well be left as a matter of opinion. We do this, sometimes, to protect against erosion—the erosion of our faith by other cultural currents. But it can be a little difficult to join Paul in being all things to all people if we are constantly concerned that we will stub our toe somewhere on Mars Hill.

I want to be like Jesus. I want to go about doing good. I want to heal people and forgive people and love people and know people. I want to say to my Father, when I come to the end, "I have finished the work you have given me to do." Also like Jesus, I want to tell stories. I want to tell them from the stage as a theatre artist. I want my stories to be a deliberate, energetic response to God and to the world around me.

# EIGHT:
## *God Speaks Through Us: Godspell—Something Happening*

*What difference does my personal rela-
tionship with God make to the possible
impact of my performance?*

In 1983 I was forty years old. I had been in theatre to some degree or other for thir-ty-four of those forty years, including earning my living acting in various parts of the United States, and once—a highlight of my life in many ways—a European tour with a show I was acting in at the time.

I have spoken of these things in greater depth in an earlier chapter. I mention them now so that you will understand that what I did in 1983 was not nothing. It was not small, and it was not insignif-icant. It was something very big and it eventually changed my life in ways I could not have imagined.

In late 1983 I became aware of an upcoming audition for an important company. I believed, for reasons that were valid for the time, that if I attended that audition I would be hired and could resume acting professionally. At that time it had been several years since I had actually earned a living from performance, although I had picked up various paying music and theatre gigs as part of my normal artist's patchwork income. I thought it would be great to have steady work in the field again. I had children ranging from "almost 3" to thirteen years old. Since theatre is primarily a night job, I could be home with them days. It seemed like a great idea, and I was sure that it would all happen if I attended this audition. Looking back, I don't know why I was so sure, but I had a great inner certainty. It may have been the enemy of our souls trying to deceive me and distract me. It may have been God offering me a perfectly legitimate human choice between flesh and spirit.

There was no sin here, but there was a choice to be made. Here's the other side of the equation: during these years I had a consuming desire to know the voice of the Lord in my life. He had given us the Disneyland trip the previous summer and I was at this time waiting, praying, seeking to know whether he was speaking to me about a trip to Israel the following spring. So far, Israel was completely without substance (as Disneyland had been the day I sat on the sofa with the Lord and gave it back to him). I knew that if I was hired by the theatre company I would be under contract during the time of the trip to Israel. I believed that if I signed a contract with the theatre company, God would simply withdraw the trip to Israel. I would have made it impossible, so it would simply not materialize.

The question was the same as before the trip to Disneyland: was I or was I not hearing the Lord's voice? Well—as regards Disneyland, obviously yes. We'd had a great vacation just a few months ago. This fact certainly boosted my confidence and strengthened my willingness to take risks. But the stakes were so much higher. With Disneyland, all I stood to lose in the "real world" was face. It would be humiliating not to go and everyone would be cruelly disappointed, apparently for no reason. But nothing else would change on the surface of life.

This time everything would change. If I was wrong about Israel I would have thrown away, for no reason, a tremendous professional opportunity. More than that, I would have severed—forever, as far as I knew—my lifelong relationship with theatre. That is how I saw it: black and white, all or nothing. I was being asked to relinquish absolutely my relationship with theatre, in order to see whether or not God was talking to me. Maybe I had a huge internal battle. But looking back, all these years later, I don't remember one. I remember it as no real contest. I walked away from theatre.

I did, indeed, go to Israel. It was an amazing trip. I was baptized in the Jordan River. I had hours of private conversation with God, deepening our relationship. I sang quietly to Him on the bus as we drove along the top of the Golan Heights.

As my life has unfolded, I can see little glimpses of why God might have taken me through this second test. The first test—giving up the Disneyland trip—was small in comparison, and the question being answered—whether or not I was hearing God—was answered immediately.

In this second test, I walked away from my life as I knew it—kind of like Abraham leaving Ur, I guess. We know the story of Abraham as all of one piece, one fabric. But Abraham experienced it in sections, the way we experience our own lives. We can look at Abraham's life and—right while we're reading about his leaving Ur—we already know about Isaac—about David—about Jesus. Abraham merely felt called out of Ur. He felt mighty uncomfortable about it sometimes, too.

I thought I would never do theatre again. I didn't for about eight years. Then a peculiar thing happened. The Lord began to restore theatre to my life for his own purposes. My hand didn't—and doesn't— close around it. The matter was settled in 1983 and my flesh has never again been tempted by it, but it is a whale of a lot of fun in the spirit to watch God pour theatre *through* me. I have received more rich joy and a deeper sense of privilege in my twenty plus years of theatre in

God's kingdom than I ever dreamed of knowing in nearly forty years of theatre in my own kingdom.

I spoke early on about God's speaking *to* us and *through* us. The Disneyland and Israel stories are examples of God's speaking *to* us. In chapter four I used the story of Gideon from the Bible to illustrate the same principle. Let us move to considering how He may speak *through* us. I want to look first at a story about Elijah from the Old Testament, and then at a production of *Godspell* I directed.

In the 18th chapter of I Kings is a passage regarding the life of Elijah in which we may find some parallels to the passage from the life of Gideon. As we join the story, there has been drought in the land of Israel for three years as prophesied by the prophet Elijah. During these three years some extraordinary things happen in Elijah's life. First, God tells him to hide himself by the Wadi Cherith. Ravens bring bread and meat twice a day, and he gets water from the wadi. Eventually, the wadi dries up. The Lord sends Elijah to a widow in Zarephath. This widow, the Lord says, has been commanded to feed Elijah. When he comes upon her, she is about to bake a small loaf of bread with her last flour and oil, to share with her son as a last meal before they both succumb to starvation. Elijah instructs her to go ahead and feed her son and herself, but first to feed him. He gives her God's promise that she will not run out of flour or oil before God sends rain. For a time they all live off the daily food she is able to prepare from the flour and oil that, true to Elijah's word, keep flowing as needed. After a time, the widow's son sickens and dies. Elijah is granted the power and privilege of restoring him to life.

Some time later God sends Elijah back to the evil King Ahab—whom he hasn't seen since announcing the start of the drought three years ago, and who has been trying in the meantime to kill Elijah. Three years of drought, some ravens, and the widow's dead son have prepared Elijah for this very public encounter with Ahab:

> …and…Ahab went to meet Elijah. When he saw Elijah, he said to him, "Is that you, you troubler of Israel?"

"I have not made trouble for Israel," Elijah replied. "But you and your father's family have. You have abandoned the Lord's commands and have followed the Baals. Now summon the people from all over Israel to meet me on Mount Carmel. And bring the four hundred and fifty prophets of Baal and the four hundred prophets of Asherah, who eat at Jezebel's table."

So Ahab sent word throughout all Israel and assembled the prophets on Mount Carmel. Elijah went before the people and said, "How long will you waver between two opinions? If the Lord is God, follow him; but if Baal is God, follow him."

But the people said nothing.

Then Elijah said to them, "I am the only one of the Lord's prophets left, but Baal has four hundred and fifty prophets. Get two bulls for us. Let them choose one for themselves, and let them cut it into pieces and put it on the wood but not set fire to it. I will prepare the other bull and put it on the wood but not set fire to it. Then you call on the name of your god, and I will call on the name of the Lord. The god who answers by fire—he is God."

Then all the people said, "What you say is good."

Elijah said to the prophets of Baal, "Choose one of the bulls and prepare it first, since there are so many of you. Call on the name of your god, but do not light the fire." So they took the bull given them and prepared it.

Then they called on the name of Baal from morning till noon. "O Baal, answer us!" they shouted. But there was no response; no one answered. And they danced around the altar they had made.

At noon Elijah began to taunt them. "Shout louder!" he said. "Surely he is a god! Perhaps he is deep in thought, or busy, or traveling. Maybe he is sleeping and must be awakened." So they shouted louder and slashed themselves with swords and spears, as was their custom, until their blood flowed. Midday passed, and they continued their frantic prophesying until the time for the evening sacrifice. But there was no response, no one answered, no one paid attention.

Then Elijah said to all the people, "Come here to me." They came to him, and he repaired the altar of the Lord, which was in ruins. Elijah took twelve stones, one for each of the tribes descended from Jacob, to whom the word of the Lord had come, saying, "Your name shall be Israel." With the stones he built an altar in the name of the Lord, and he dug a trench around it large enough to hold two seahs of seed. He arranged the wood, cut the bull into pieces and laid it on the wood. Then he said to them, "Fill four large jars with water and pour it on the offering and on the wood."

"Do it again," he said, and they did it again.

"Do it a third time," he ordered, and they did it the third time. The water ran down around the altar and even filled the trench.

At the time of sacrifice, the prophet Elijah stepped forward and prayed, "O Lord, God of Abraham, Isaac and Israel, let it be known today that you are God in Israel and that I am your servant and have done all these things at your command. Answer me, O Lord, answer me, so these people will know that you, O Lord, are God, and that you are turning their hearts back again."

Then the fire of the Lord fell and burned up the sacrifice, the wood, the stones and the soil, and also licked up the water in the trench.

When all the people saw this, they fell prostrate and cried, "The Lord—he is God! The Lord—he is God!" (I Kings 18:16-39).

You will recall that Gideon prepared an offering for the angel of the Lord, the angel of the Lord consumed it, and Gideon thereby knew that he had, indeed, been dealing with the angel of the Lord. As far as we know, no one else was present for this transaction.

As far as we know, only Elijah was present when the ravens fed him, and only the widow and her son were present in Elijah's transactions with them. However, on top of Mount Carmel we find Ahab, Elijah, four hundred fifty prophets of Baal, four hundred prophets of Asherah *and* the people of Israel! This is going to be a real dog and pony show.

First, the prophets of Baal prepare a sacrifice. Baal doesn't show up. It may be worth considering that this may have been unusual. Baal is a servant of Satan, and we know that Satan is capable of interacting in colorful and powerful ways with his worshippers and servants. If Baal doesn't show up on this occasion, it may be because he is prevented from doing so, and this may be part of what Elijah is counting on from the Lord.

When Elijah's turn comes, he insists on doing everything himself. He has stated that he alone is a prophet of the Lord, and so he alone carries out the Lord's task. There are four hundred fifty prophets of Baal to prepare their offering. Elijah alone builds an altar of stone, piles wood on it, digs a trench around it, cuts up the bull and arranges it on the wood. There is great and meaningful symbolism involved—twelve stones for the twelve tribes, twelve jars of water (four jars times three). Oh, and the people are allowed to pour the water. The doubters are often the ones assigned to pour cold water on the sacrifice!

When Gideon made his offering, the angel of the Lord responded with fire, consuming the entire offering. Gideon may have *hoped* that would happen. Elijah *knew*. He called on the name of the Lord expecting that the Lord would answer in a way that demonstrated to the people that the Lord was, indeed, God.

God moved Gideon to prepare an offering so that Gideon might come to know God. It was a part of Gideon's preparation and consecration to God's service. God moved Elijah to prepare an offering to refute the lies of the enemy and restore the hearts of the people, in repentance, to God.

God continues to operate in both these ways in the lives of his people. In my life. In yours, if you want.

In spring of 2001 I directed a production of *Godspell* for the university where I teach. *Godspell* is written for a cast of ten. We used eighteen. The show's original company used its own names for character names—except for Jesus and Judas—and I chose to keep that practice (and carry it one step further by not designating Judas by name). This decision helped immediately to loosen and communalize the sense of ownership of the show, although nearly doubling the cast size created a fairly intense and delicate piece of work in assigning lines and solos in a balanced and personalized way.

As the director of theatre in a Christian liberal arts university, I am profoundly interested in understanding and encouraging the integration of artistry with the Christian faith. Performing arts either can exist for the glory of God or they cannot. If they cannot, a Christian has no business in the performing arts. This question is a centuries old tension within the church. I believe performance *can* glorify God. At its most basic level, that phenomenon occurs at the same place as any other human activity from cooking to reading to fixing the drain: it takes place in the intention of the performer. If I genuinely *prefer* God's glory to my own, God honors that fact and is honored by it.

During the rehearsal process, I spoke with the cast about the sixth chapter of Judges, where Gideon encounters the angel of the Lord. I spoke with them also about Elijah on the top of Mount Carmel.

I said to my students, "I am praying that each of you will have a Gideon encounter with God during our rehearsal process, an encounter that will change you so that when you step on stage to perform *Godspell,* God will be able to ignite our offering and reveal himself as he chooses to the people in our audience."

After that we encountered difficulties. Our lighting system failed, and we had to send it several states away for repairs during spring break. Our normal channels of communication with the public dried up for budget reasons beyond our control, so that we were afraid no one would hear about the show.

We began to tithe our time to prayer. At the beginning of each three hour rehearsal, we spent twenty minutes in prayer. The difficulties continued. Someone's grandmother died. Someone's good friend from high school, a young woman of nineteen or twenty, died of illness. One cast member's dear cousin died in a tragic accident. We continued to pray for twenty minutes before each rehearsal. Our lights came back fixed. Reservations started coming in. We felt the comfort and presence of the Lord in all our difficulties. Twenty minutes of prayer isn't a lot. But twenty minutes several times a week faithfully over many weeks was a new experience for some of our students. Prayer is intangible, and there is no clinical proof that the Lord blessed us in specific ways. But we believed he did.

Opening night we were a quarter of an hour late starting the show. At curtain time I said to the audience, "We have a wonderful pianist, but she isn't here yet. Will you pray with me?" They did. When she arrived, it turned out that a cat, a rabbit, and finally a fox had run in front of her car at various points on her trip, slowing her down. While she was stopped at a light, a drunken man walked in front of her car and collapsed! She didn't know what to do—surely it looked as if she had hit him, and it would be inappropriate to leave. But a uniformed policeman with no visible car nearby just happened to be standing on the corner. He strolled over and said, "I saw the whole thing. You didn't do anything wrong. I'll take care of it. You go on." I'd love to know what time *that* was! We prayed at 7:30; she arrived, we prayed again and started the show—our orchestra now intact—at 7:45.

As the run continued, we had such large crowds that we had to turn away dozens of people from the door. From those who actually saw the performance, one of the most common responses was, "This was a worship experience." Worship takes place in the present, and cannot properly be restructured for later spectatorship. Theatre characteristically makes use of the "illusion of the first time." But worship is not an illusion. It is an active engagement with a living God.

While we were mounting *Godspell,* I operated on the assumption that our process was unique to that play and that time. As I have contemplated our work later, and the comments of the audience,

I wonder. Is it possible God intends for the time commitment to prayer, the absence of illusion, and the presence of—something real?—to characterize our work as Christian theatre artists?

Wole Soyinka, the Pulitzer prize winning Nigerian playwright, says that Yoruba tragedy is not "about something happening. It *is something happening."* I consider the differences in perception of Holy Communion/the Eucharist/the Lord's Table as presented by various denominations within the Body of Christ. In some, it is purely a commemorative occasion. In others, the Real Presence of Christ is claimed in the elements of bread and wine, changing the perception of sacredness surrounding the occasion.

I shared my thoughts about Soyinka with a friend from Kenya. He said, "Is that the theory underlying your production of *Godspell?* Because I came to watch a play. But I got caught up in something happening—and that something was worship."

I sometimes tell my students that the way we treat each other in rehearsals—even early in the process—affects God's possibilities for blessing the little old lady in the back row on Thursday night of the second week of the run. Doing flows from being, and process *is* product.

Is it possible for theatre always to be, not "about something happening," but *something happening?*

# NINE:
## The Underground God

*Living in a society that is so touchy and standoffish about God—especially my God—how can I do my work in a way that presents Him as inviting, alive and vital—all the things I know Him to be?*

Researchers who attempt to find the roots of theatre often connect it with storytelling and with tribal religious ritual. We understand the storytelling. Our near and dear still walk in the door after being gone hunting for several autumn days and say, "I was *this close* to bagging a five point buck!" We don't seem to understand the religious ritual as well. Most people who write about these rituals talk about fertility and life cycles, and they talk about them in ways that suggest that the people involved in the rituals were inventing ways to attempt to control their environment. There is an implicit assumption that the ritual participants were barking up the wrong tree, that all their actions were purely symbolic, were unsophisticated and—well—yes, in a pejorative way—"primitive." There is a further implicit assumption that we know better now. I have not encountered any research that suggests that these people groups were actually engaged in interaction with real spiritual forces. The research may exist, but it isn't showing up in main stream theatre history texts with which I am acquainted.

I began to question current contemporary thought when I encountered a book on theatrical roots of near Eastern cultures of antiquity—Canaanite, Hittite, Egyptian. The book discussed the rituals of these people groups, quoting from their sacred texts. I was reading along about these rituals—specifically the human behavior and actions within those rituals—and I am so accustomed to contemporary rhetoric that I was going right along with the flow. Then the writer began to discuss the Israelites in the same vein, quoting from *their* sacred texts—in this case, Psalms. I sort of woke up with a little start. I thought, "Yes, but you see, *these* people were actually *doing* something. They were actually engaged in a dialogue with a spiritual entity. *Something real was happening.*" Suddenly it hit me. Maybe they were *all* engaged in dialogues with spiritual entities. Maybe they were *all* doing *something real*.

The Israelites alone were engaged with the Lord. The Lord is the creator, sustainer and ruler of all creation. But the Lord does not deny the existence of other gods. His book is crawling with them—Old and New Testaments. In fact, two of the key stories in the narrative involve encounters with the Great Pretender—the enemy of our souls, Satan himself. The first encounter is with Adam and Eve—the first Adam—in the Garden of Eden at the time of the fall of man. The second is with the last Adam—Jesus—in the desert at the time of the temptations of Christ just before Jesus began his three years of concentrated earthly ministry.

False gods do not sit around doing nothing. They are not false because they "don't exist." They are false because they are not God. They are active, and they are interactive—not the wood and stone idols, obviously, but the lying spirits behind them. Paul speaks of Satan as like a roaring lion prowling about seeking whom he may devour. If he is doing that in our world, it seems likely he was doing it among the Canaanites, Hittites, Egyptians and Israelites, too.

If we know that the Israelites were engaged in a real dialogue with the real God, the Lord, and if surrounding peoples were engaged in *similar* rituals with *similar texts,* isn't it at least possible that they were also engaged in real dialogue with Baal—Asherah—Satan?

I am in a kind of brainstorming session all by myself here. I am not a historian. I am conjecturing in a very free form *not* in order to nail down what the ancient past looked like, but in order to open some channels of thought regarding possibilities for the present.

Two of the strong probable roots of theatre, as I have said, are story and ritual. If ancient rituals may have been, not merely a kind of primitive wishful thinking, but actual interactions between flesh and spirit, then Wole Soyinka may have been onto something. Maybe not only Yoruba tragedy but theatre in general is invited to be not merely *about something happening*, but *something happening*. If the altar in the middle of the Greek stages refers to an actual *something happening* within the performances, no wonder we are unable to capture the splendor, the majesty, the flavor of what the Greeks were doing. In our day, we can only imitate their conjectured form—or create our own. But if we are way out in left field about the actual content and its intention, no wonder we cannot find the life in the form.

Was ancient ritual designed to put the people back in right relationship with the god? If they had the wrong god, it would be impossible to get in right relationship. Right relationship can be achieved only with the right God.

Contemporary western society is in a terrible pickle because we don't even have the *wrong* God these days. We're trying to operate without one. We allowed Nietzsche to declare him dead and we have allowed contemporary academics and others to throw dirt on his grave. But that hasn't actually killed him. It has merely sent the search for him underground, in theatre as elsewhere. The spiritual nature has always been tasteless, colorless and odorless, and we have recently changed our vocabulary so that this nature is barely perceptible to the naked ear. I do not believe the search for God is gone; I believe it has merely been rephrased.

Humanity longs for community and for salvation—for a deep and completing experience of the self and of the other. In this search, performers are among the vanguard, inventing and articulating the codes by which we conduct the search. Without a common societal vocabulary for the holy (and we haven't had one since the first World War), the artists' work of exploration becomes more intricate, more significant. The temptation to reflect chaos for its own sake is great. But we are not made in the image of fallenness. We are fallen—but we are made in the image of God, and it is that image we seek as Christian artists—as the deer pants for streams of water (Psalm 42:1).

When Jesus was about to begin his public ministry, the enemy came to him. When we find the work to which we are truly called, we also encounter the opposition of the enemy. The enemy has gone to some lengths to control theatre and to cheapen its reputation *because of the power of story*. If we feel called and hope to be used in this field, we will be offered the choices Jesus was offered in the desert.

"The devil said to him, 'If you are the Son of God, tell this stone to become bread" (Luke 4:3). This is the invitation to exert *our own power* in *our own behalf* to meet *our own need*. There appears to be nothing wrong with this course of action on the face of it. Really, why shouldn't Jesus turn the stone into bread? The forty day fast is over. He's hungry. Why shouldn't he? There is a mystery here. On other occasions, Jesus turns water to wine, multiplies bread and fish, and causes the fishing apostles to net an enormous catch. But at this moment he refuses to turn the stone to bread. Perhaps it is because the only reason to do so would be to accommodate, in accord with his own will, his own flesh. In some ways, this is a human right. But human rights are relinquished, are exercised only under the direction of the Lord when we have responded to the call of the Lord.

> The devil led him up to a high place and showed him in an instant all the kingdoms of the world. And he said to him, "I will give

you all their authority and splendor, for it has been given to me, and I can give it to anyone I want to. So if you worship me, it will all be yours."

Jesus answered, "It is written: 'Worship the Lord your God and serve him only'" (Luke 4:5-8).

This is a short cut. Seeing, in the distance, that which is truly meant to be our own, we are invited to reach for it by forbidden means. Kierkegaard says, in *Purity of Heart*:

> There is only one means and there is only one end: the means and the end are one and the same thing. There is only one end: the genuine good; and only one means: this, to be willing to use those means which genuinely are good—but the genuine good is precisely the end. In time one distinguishes between the two and considers that the end is more important than the means. One thinks that the end is the main thing and demands of one who is striving that he reach the end. He need not be so particular about the means. Yet this is not so, and to gain an end in this fashion is an unholy act of impatience.

And so we find that, operating as the called, every step we take toward the goal impacts the potential for full realization of the goal—affirms or changes, in fact, the substance of the goal.

> The devil led him to Jerusalem and had him stand on the highest point of the temple. "If you are the Son of God," he said, "throw yourself down from here. For it is written: 'He will command his angels concerning you to guard you carefully; they will lift you up in their hands, so that you will not strike your foot against a stone.'" (Luke 4:9-11).

This is the invitation to use God's own words, God's own promises, against God—to demand our legal rights. It is an invitation to insist on living under the law instead of risking everything on God's grace and goodness.

> Jesus answered, "It says: 'Do not put the Lord your God to the test.'" Jesus returned to Galilee in the power of the Spirit, and news about him spread through the whole countryside. He taught in their synagogues, and everyone praised him (Luke 4:12, 14-15).

If we avoid these temptations to provide for our own needs, to take illicit short cuts, and to test God, often we, too, may have the power of the Spirit in us and be praised by everyone. But we do these things simply, as child, as storyteller. Otherwise, they miss their mark and the people go away empty, whether or not they realize it. As actors—storytellers—the story is our home base. We find the truth in the stories we tell, and we intentionally connect it to the larger truth from which all truth flows. We pray for something real to happen—on the stage, in the filming—ultimately, in and for the audience.

I think of a tiny baby gazing raptly into the face of her mother, smiling and cooing. The coos do not sound much like our speech, but we gaze back in uninterrupted delight. I think we gaze, as artists, into the mysterious, loving face of the Father, smiling back at him, and all the most splendid creative work we produce is nothing more than our baby coos, not sounding much like his speech—but precious, enrapturing and utterly wonderful in his sight because of his great love for us.

# TEN:
## *Fame—Smoke or Mirrors?*

*What do I say when people think I'm really good?*

Sometimes success comes. In the fallen world's theatre, success can lead to dismay because even people whose whole life appears to be lived attending to the flesh have a Martha nature and a Mary nature—a nature more concerned with the external rewards of doing and a nature more concerned with the internal rewards of being. The exciting pungency of success, however, does not meet anyone's spiritual needs. This discovery can be very disturbing.

As believers, trying to stay centered on Christ and keep a godly perspective can be demanding. Success is a rush, and it is seductive. I want everyone to think I'm wonderful, but then I feel guilty for thinking about myself all the time! What do we do with the praise? As a young Christian, I was both more full of pride and more afraid of being thought proud than I am now. I was taught that I should immediately pass all praise to the Lord—verbally. But it feels cheesy to all the time be saying, "It wasn't me. It was Jesus. Praise God." In fact, we don't much say that. But we are uncomfortable with the praise. It feels like the fans think they're getting something from *us*—something we know in our hearts we don't have available to give them. On the other hand, when I tried to turn people's shy and delighted compliments towards God, with words, in that moment their faces always fell, looking slightly disappointed, as though I had refused a gift. In fact, I had.

As my own faith and artistry have matured, I have learned that there are basically two kinds of people who compliment my performances. The first kind is people who already know that God is entitled to receive all the glory, and their praising me is part of their glorifying Him. With these people it is appropriate to smile and say thank you. The other group is generally younger spiritually and may not have yet grasped the Allness of God. They aren't going to grasp it in this brief interaction with me, either, and with them, too, it is appropriate to smile and say thank you. I have learned that God Himself will intervene and let me know when I am talking to that rare and occasional person who will be blessed by my saying something else. Then I say whatever He suggests. In any case, I have noticed that all these people pigheadedly insist on continuing to think me wonderful, after a show, no matter how articulately I attempt to correct them! I finally figured out that, as long as **I** don't get confused about which one is God and which one is me, it probably isn't necessary that I try to straighten out the rest of the world in a few minutes backstage.

What goes on *in my own mind* may differ somewhat from what goes on in my actual conversations with those who appreciate my work. There's nothing wrong with this, and my own internal process continues to grow as I draw nearer to the Lord, as will yours. A number of years ago I taught a study for a group of friends on the subject of how to meditate in scripture. In preparing for class one day I encountered this passage:

> Durig harvest time, three of the thirty chief men came down to David at the cave of Adullam, while a band of Philistines was encamped in the Valley of Rephaim. At that time David was in the stronghold, and the Philistine garrison was at Bethlehem. David longed for water and said, "Oh, that someone would get me a drink of water from the well near the gate of Bethlehem!" So the three mighty men broke through the Philistine lines, drew water from the well near the gate of Bethlehem and carried it back to David. But he refused to drink it; instead, he poured it out before the Lord. "Far be it from me, O Lord, to do this!" he said, "Is it not the blood of men who went at the risk of their lives?" And David would not drink it (2 Samuel 23:13-17).

This brief account is in the middle of a chapter that brags about the deeds of David's mighty men, and these three in particular. The stories read like Tall Tales of individual heroes overcoming mythic odds. In the middle of this account comes this small, personal episode.

I found it odd and perhaps petty of David not to drink the water. I didn't understand why he would make that choice, but I brushed the matter aside, in a hurry to finish my preparations for class! In class, someone said, "Why would David do that? It doesn't seem very considerate, after his men went to all that trouble."

"Oh, Sandy!" I said. "I am so sorry! I think God tried to tell me this question would come up, but I was in a hurry and brushed past it, and now I don't know the answer. Let's ask him to tell us right now." We all prayed, and God did give us an answer. I am sure there are many lessons in this passage of scripture, but this is what we understood that day.

"Why would those men do this?" God seemed to ask us. David was just daydreaming—he didn't expect anyone to do anything. He didn't think there was anything to be done. We can imagine his three good buddies getting together in a corner of the cave to murmur over his words. In a wash of youthful exuberance they decide, "Let's do it!" So they sneak out, break into the Philistine camp and bring the water to David, feeling pretty dadgum cocky and hoping to hand David a laugh, as well as elicit his admiration. All right, so it was a crazy stunt. But they got away with it, so no harm done, right?

Wrong. David discerned harm in it. What harm? Well, why would these men do this? What does it indicate about their regard for David that they would undertake such a fool's errand?

Hero worship. Hero worship can be benign or it can be malignant. Hero worship is a normal and expected phase in the growth and development of young people. I adored my eighth grade math teacher. Because of that rosy glow, I got a lot better at math, after stinking at it in younger years. I have enjoyed the math related aspects of my life—regular stuff like balancing my checkbook or designing a departmental budget—all my adult life because of that crush as a twelve or thirteen-year-old on a junior high school teacher. Because of him, I played math games with my children on automobile trips and *they* like math. Crazy. Nice man. Hero worship is developmentally appropriate, benign and useful.

What happens if the heroes try to receive the worship? A lot of movie stars' and rock stars' lives crash and burn. Is there a cause and effect related to the heroes' interactions with their publics? Maybe, maybe not. It does seem that the big Hollywood names who seem to maintain their dignity and self respect do so by distancing themselves from the hue and cry, by not believing their own press—good or bad. This is healthy and sensible, and can protect the hero to some extent.

I believe David went a step further. He wasn't merely a hero chosen of men. He was a leader chosen of God. He took the offering and poured it out as an offering to the Lord. By risking their lives, the men had offered their lives to David in the water they brought. David took the offering and passed it to the Lord, the only one worthy to receive it. In this way, he protected himself from blasphemy, and he protected his men from worshipping false gods. Because the offering reached its rightful destination, no harm was done. The passage doesn't say what the three mighty men did in response to David's pouring the water as a libation before the Lord. Hopefully, they worshipped God with him.

May we go and do likewise? When praise is offered to us, may we pass it to the Father of light, from whom comes every good and perfect gift? One does not have the impression that David necessarily rebuked or offered correction to his men. He took the offering from their hands and passed it on to the only one deserving it. If we are walking with the Lord, he will give us discernment in the moment to know what to do with the praise we are offered. In this way we, too, may hope to bless both God and our admirers.

If we think about it, isn't hero worship the most natural thing in the world? We are made in the image of God. If we are even remotely operating within that image, well then, naturally—*naturally*—we can be mistaken for God. The great thing is not to mistake *ourselves* for him. Lucifer seems to have done something like that, and all hell broke loose.

# ELEVEN:
## *Community*

*What is community? How am I supposed to integrate it with my life as a Christian and as an artist?*

Theatrical production is known for collaboration—for community. Community is one of the chief hungers of our nature and one of the main attractions of theatre—for artist and audience.

Jerry and I returned to San Francisco after our year in Minneapolis with the Firehouse Theatre. We were exhilarated from our success at earning a living as actors, and awed by the amazing experience of having performed in Europe! But we were also restless and homesick. Augustine says the heart is restless until it finds its rest in God. But in those days I did not yet know that. So we came home to

San Francisco hoping to find what still seemed to be missing from our lives.

Our friend, Paul Rebillot, who taught theatre at Stanford, was putting together a group of people to do Greek theatre on the Stanford campus in the summer of 1969. At the same time, other friends with other interests invited us to go homesteading with them in Canada! Both these ventures were communal, and both were deeply attractive to us. Eventually, the artist in us won out and we decided to work with Paul.

As it turned out, the Stanford project never materialized. A group of us followed Paul to Ashland, Oregon, where he was working with the Shakespeare Festival for a month. We camped on a mountain and got to know each other, having acting workshops with Paul on the side of the mountain when he had breaks from the Festival schedule.

When we returned to the Bay Area there were still thirty or so of us living in a tiny house in Cotati (about 80 miles north of San Francisco) and trying to put together a theatre company. In the fall, we found a twelve bedroom, five bath Victorian mansion in

San Francisco, with a ballroom in the basement! It was in Pacific Heights, overlooking the San Francisco marina and the Golden Gate Bridge. We negotiated a lease, and twenty-four of us moved in, forming the Gestalt Fool Theatre Family.

We rehearsed in the basement ballroom, doing original works by our members. They were well received by audiences, although we never earned a living performing. The hippie revolution was emerging in the culture of San Francisco—flowers in gun barrels, Timothy Leary, along with the Black Panthers and Altamont. We performed in lodge halls and church basements. Sometimes we were invited to the local dance emporiums, the Fillmore and Avalon Ballrooms, where we did interactive improvisation with the audience between rock groups. Our theatre was social, political and experimental. It was moderately successful.

Our family life, on the other hand, was wildly successful. We had family meetings incessantly to iron out problems; we experimented with rolfing (a form of deep tissue massage), co-counseling, and Primal Scream therapy. We had a Tai Chi master come to the house to give us our own class, since there were so many of us. For six weeks an Italian journalist stayed with us writing a feature article on us for a European magazine. Other communities in the San Francisco area came to ask us how we were structured, hoping to improve their own communities.

I think our success was based on love—on our willingness to agree, even in the toughest conflicts, that the other person was probably doing the best they could. Community, I think, is a four syllable word for love. God is love, and the Trinity is a community. Our rehearsals were constantly interrupted by family matters, but, since we considered ourselves all one family, that was not fatally disruptive. Because we lived together, we found other rehearsal times to make up for the lost ones.

Living together with such a large number of people took so much energy that we only lasted as a theatre company for about three years. But many of us are still in touch; our children are friends. We gather occasionally from around the country—around the world—for a weekend. A few of us have made our way as professional artists. Two of us have become doctors, and pretty much all of us have maintained a concern for the welfare of humanity. Once you get used to thinking about other people, it feels right to continue. We are made that way.

My son Ryan once wrote: "God is a communal being, and His community is an integral part of His creativity....In fact, the Hebrew word transliterated *Elohiym*, and generally translated 'God' in the Bible, is really a plural word..." So, then, we may say God is plural all by themself? How singular! Humankind is like God in this way. Each tiny one of us is made in the image of God—and it takes all of us even to begin to reflect that image. We reflect the image of God communally every time we collaborate. A barn raising, a quilting bee—these "old fashioned" activities are recognized as communal. Even cleaning house together can birth the deep sense of well being that we experience in community. In today's busy, urban life we may find community sorting clothes at a clothing bank or serving a meal at a shelter. Community is sharing—sharing of faith, work, life. We are drawn to it because it reflects the Trinity. It cannot take the place of our relationship with God, although sometimes we may drift into letting it seem to do so. That can be idolatry. But we are made for the intimacy of community and, as theatre artists, we find much intimacy through our work. Maintaining a strong personal relationship with Christ helps us to savor community thoroughly without giving it a place it isn't meant for and can't fill in our lives.

Ryan speaks of community as being an integral part of man's artistic creativity as well as God's. Ryan discusses what he calls *direct* and *indirect* community. Direct community he describes as what happens in deliberate collaboration on a joint project—the exchange and refinement of ideas that results in a better project than anyone could have produced alone. Indirect community he ascribes to the creative influence of those who have gone before us creatively.

Another helpful set of terms might be *conscious* and *unconscious* community. Conscious community is our deliberate interaction with the work of others—either our collaboration in the moment as we work together, or our references, internal or external, to the known work of others preceding or contemporary to us. Unconscious community would take us into the realm of Jung's collective unconscious, or race memory, where many things are described as known to us that are not yet recollected. I can't help wondering whether Jung was trying, without reference to Christ, to come to terms with the cloud of witnesses in Romans 12. Madeleine L'Engle (who is certainly part of my conscious community, though I have not met her outside her pages) reminds me that writing is often a process of remembrance—not the remembrance of facts, necessarily, but the remembrance of truth. Jung seemed tapped into the same idea.

The Colorado Christian University production of *Godspell,* too, was an experience of both direct and indirect conscious community—this time within the Body of Christ. No doubt it was also an experience of unconscious community, and I will attempt to talk about that, too. Obviously, it will be harder to talk about.

The script of *Godspell* reads somewhat like an ordinary script and somewhat like a *commedia scenario.* It is filled with parenthetical expressions of the playwright's intent, along with phrases such as "While it is not necessary to follow this direction literally...", or "These divisions are arbitrary and could be switched in other productions...". So I felt well within appropriate artistic boundaries in saying to the cast, "This play was written in and for the '70s, and all its incidental humor is slanted in that direction. I want you to update it so that it feels contemporary to your peers." They began tentatively to insert one-liners from commercials, movies and television. As I affirmed their work, they grew more adventurous, changing a Peter Lorre image used in the original script to Austin Powers, changing a Three Stooges sight gag to *The Matrix*.

These experiments took place within the framework of rehearsal. Some of them would be one-liners designed by one person to elicit a laugh based on the collective audience recognition of a popular cultural reference. This indirect community experience of one actor's creativity became a direct community involvement through the response of the rehearsing company and, eventually, the audience.

All these forms of interaction are common to theatrical process. We are taking them apart here so that we may see how natural and common—available to all of us—the creative process is. Everyone experiences multiple moments of creativity within the course of a day. They are pleasurable and of value in and of themselves. Artists consciously mold these moments into an order that helps us all to discern the cosmos within our own chaos.

Even the prayer times were a form of conscious community within the *Godspell* process—although they were the moments, you may say, at which we consciously invited unconscious community! It is possible to invite the cloud of witnesses to join us. Doing so does not guarantee, or even necessarily suggest, that we will recognize them when they do— and perhaps "cloud of witnesses" is merely the most identifiable metaphor I have available as a Christian for the concept of unconscious community.

I know that we couldn't fix our lights; they were fixed.

I know that we couldn't fill our houses; they were filled to overflowing—running over.

I know that we had no pianist at curtain time opening night; she came.

I do not know of anything we did that may have influenced these outcomes—except prayer. We believe prayer *did* influence them. Can community be direct and conscious and clothed in mystery? Yes.

Community is one of the most attractive aspects of theatre, for both theatre artists and audience. Theatre is probably the only art form that *cannot* be practiced in solitude. It *requires* community. As humans created in the image of God, we crave community. Community is an expression of yes. It affirms being and frees doing. Watch the Academy Awards. Some winners just stand up with a list of people it would be rude to forget to thank. Others are overwhelmed in the moment of accepting the award—overwhelmed by the *randomness* of their being chosen to stand there when the whole project could never have taken place at all without the contribution of every single person involved!

In an improv class we learn that the basis of improv is yes. "Find a way to say yes to anything that happens in the improv. That's how to keep it going." More, that's how to keep a creative environment alive. We speak of needing to feel "safe" in order to work well creatively. That is because we must fail repeatedly in order to succeed. But only *doing* can fail. *Being* doesn't fail. Being just *is*. A properly functioning creative community knows how to say no to things I am *doing* without in any way accosting my *being*. Because it is safe, my being does not begin to shrink, but instead flourishes. I can continue new ways of doing until something I do also receives a yes.

Ideally, for beginning artists, this safety is provided by the director or instructor. The members of a class will learn and mirror the attitude of the instructor. In a beginning acting class, at first I allow only positive feedback. Most of us have learned at a startlingly young age how to find fault, how to articulate what we don't like. It is challenging and worthwhile to train ourselves diligently to look for the good, and to learn how to phrase rich acknowledgments, compliments, affirmations. It is possible to do this even in an environment where the director or instructor is not modeling positive reinforcement. Daring to speak the good can go a long way towards mitigating some of the negative effects of unbalanced fault finding.

Eventually, adults in any walk of life should reach a place of internal balance wherein they provide their own safety, the yes to their own being. But every time we try something new, we will look outside ourselves to find a yes for what we are doing. Finding the place of yes is finding community. Community with God and self is the deepest yes. Other community is layered into that.

I might warn you that it is possible, to some degree and temporarily, to form community in a setting that violates conscience. If we are attempting to walk in holiness and purity before the Lord but are in artistic community with people whose personal morals differ from ours, it is tempting to abuse grace, to slip the leash of our convictions in order to protect our sense of human comraderie. There are times in any life when one will want to steal something, or gossip about absent friends, or sleep with a significant other.

Among Christians, hopefully, you will have help fighting these impulses. Outside Christianity, you are walking with people who may not even want to consider these behaviors wrong. That is why community with God (interaction with God) and with self (maintenance of personal integrity) is first.

There is an old, anonymous saying, "If, then, ye are intent upon wisdom, a lamp will not be wanting, a shepherd will not fail, and a fountain will not dry up." This is true and if you are, indeed, intent on wisdom, you will not be able to continue comfortably in the wrong direction. God can get your attention. But you have to want him to.

The Gestalt Fool was not Christian, yet the nature of true community is rooted in love, and that root flowered in our relationships even in the midst of many misunderstandings about how to live. The *Godspell* company was a Christian university theatre company. It was not designed for long life, yet the impact of our community will affect our entire lives. Putting other people's interests ahead of our own is powerful. Community is powerful—and is one of the strongest safeguards, within the performing arts, against the pride that can follow success as a performer.

# TWELVE: *Servanthood*

## *Servitude?*

$\mathcal{S}$ ervanthood. I like servanthood better. Servitude seems ignominious, graceless, involuntary. It brings to mind great sorrow such as the shame of the Middle Passage—not the shame *felt* by the Africans, for whom it was no shame—but the *real* shame of the Europeans, who lacked the grace to know their own culpability.

Servanthood, on the other hand, carries dignity—it is robed, clothed, invested—hooded. One assumes the hood of the servant. Jesus assumed it and, as we begin to lean towards him, we fall into it as well. Well, maybe not "as well" as he does it. But "as" well—as if it were well, and it is.

I learned, years ago, that in Philippians 2, two words are used that are translated "form." One means passing appearance; the other means essential nature. The word for essential nature was used to describe Jesus in the form of a servant. Servanthood is part of his essential nature. So, since we know that when we see him we shall be like him, servanthood is also a part of our essential nature. It isn't just something we try to put up with here and now until we can be released from it. It is something our deep nature seeks, something we will immerse ourselves in more and more fully as, one degree of glory at a time, we are changed to his likeness.

The entertainment industry does not encourage us to *be* servants—it encourages us to *have* servants. But artistry is not the entertainment industry, though parts of both are intricately intertwined. That is, both the artistry and the industry work themselves out through the same doings. Artistry helps make us in the image of God. Through the courtesy of Romans 8:28, wherein all things work to the good of those who love God and are the called according to his purpose, the entertainment industry also works for our good, while sometimes promoting another agenda—fame and fortune.

What *is* servanthood? Surprisingly, it isn't always making the coffee. Sometimes it is drinking the perhaps unwanted coffee that has been made. I had a rich experience of both community and servanthood in an unexpected way one winter.

In February, shortly after our production of *A Midsummer Night's Dream* closed, I had sudden, near emergency surgery to remove my gall bladder, which was a mess of infection. The last time I had been overnight in a hospital had been when I had my tonsils out at the age of eleven. Mostly, I remembered ice cream, jello, and a lot of extra attention.

But this was jarring. I have a new comprehension of the word invasive. I was over sixty; I lived alone; and when I came home I was medicated and frightened. I have a son and daughter in town; the daughter was a busy teacher and the son was a busy newlywed. I wanted, needed them to be there for me, of course. To be my son and daughter. And they were. Are. But I didn't want them to have to be, to do *everything*—and I knew I was very needy, indeed.

I had met weekly with four young women for the previous three years, since most of them were

freshmen. Each of them came into my life by way
of theatre—loving theatre and relishing artistry. As
they moved through college, God drew their atten-
tions elsewhere, to other plans He had for them that
they joyously embraced. But the friendships held.
The love and the caring held, even without doing
shows together very often. We continued to meet
weekly, to pray and to share our lives. In my need
that early spring semester, they folded about me like
the petals of a soft and fragrant flower. For an entire
week after I came home from surgery, they took
charge of my home. They cooked, they cleaned,
they brought books and studied and prayed. They
spent the night. They made a schedule and traded
me off among themselves for a week, threading my
needs through classes, work and other commitments
of their lives. A couple of times two of them were
there at the same time, but mostly they came alone,
in shifts, meeting only as they came and went. But
one of them was always there, 24/7. They didn't get
much from me that I was aware of. I was medicated,
in pain and self absorbed. But later, when I tried
to find words to thank them, one of them said, "I

loved it. It was so great to have a chance to see you in your home among your own things—to see who you are, how you are." Who knew? I have seldom felt so unavailable in my life. But God poured his ineffable elixir into the mix and presto, my need became a service.

These human exchanges of ordinary life become the ground of our character and the basis of our artistry. If I refuse to serve, considering it beneath my importance, I close the door on the very richness that I am seeking. To become first I must habitually make myself last, until I find my greatest joy in doing so.

Performing artists are often referred to as self serving. Are we? If so, is it because it is the nature of the art, or is it that a lot of self serving people are called to the appearance of the art? Have you ever had someone say, "Oh, you're an actor? Must be nice. I have to *work* for a living!" The appearance of the art of acting is that it isn't work. Lazy, self-serving people are drawn to that which isn't work. When they find out it is work, they either continue to try to avoid work, or they fall in love with the work, like the rest of us, and stay to serve it.

There are four areas of service a Christian actor may want to consider: serving God, serving theatre, serving the audience, serving one another. Each of these forms of service is addressed through process and product.

Serving God is primary in every Christian's life. Whether we eat or drink, or whatever we do, we are enjoined to do it to the glory of God (1 Cor. 10:31). The Greek word rendered as glory suggests also dignity, honor, praise and worship. So when we accept work as an actor, we must consider whether the product—the production—will have the possibility of honoring—of glorifying—God. There are no obvious answers to this question, although you will be told that there are. In fact, there are *very few* theatre productions that *intentionally dishonor* God. They don't always succeed. There are more, although still a slender minority, that *openly state* an intention to honor God. They don't always succeed, either. And there are thousands of others. You may want to ask yourself:

What is this play saying?

Is it worth saying?

Can I give myself to what this play is saying without betraying myself?

You will also want to know what the director thinks the play is saying and what the production concept is. If you know and trust the director, you may not need to pursue these questions vigorously in each case before committing to the production.

Having decided that a potential product is worth your contribution (hardly any of us thinks, consciously, in these terms, sometimes even well into our careers, but they are questions we should consider prayerfully—only God has a clear answer), you want to consider process. We don't so much need to consider general rehearsal process, over which we have no control. What we want to consider is our private, internal process. Kierkegaard's statement that the means and the end are the same thing bears a great deal of thought. How do I want to conduct my life so that the greatest possible glory for God results from my artistry?

Many artists today believe in art for art's sake. There is much value in this viewpoint, but not as a *primary* focus. If we allow ourselves to slip away from God as a primary focus, we are in very real danger of worshipping art, instead. This is such a likely mistake for humans to make that it may be the very thing God is warning us about in the 2$^{nd}$ commandment. I think of the Ten Commandments as the Top Ten Things people are likely to think of as Good Ideas that are actually Dreadful Ideas. The book of Proverbs tells us there is a way that seems right to a man, the end whereof is destruction. Perhaps the Ten Commandments help us to identify these ways that are destructive. God, knowing the backlash from these actions, graciously warns us, "Don't go there."

If art, like everything else, is primarily for God's sake, benefit or honor, then in what ways may I lawfully, pleasantly and joyfully serve art through my acting? To know the answer to this question, we must know what art is. According to the dictionary, art is "the use of the imagination to make things of aesthetic significance," including the techniques and theory involved, and including the things themselves. Aesthetics, again from the dictionary, concerns the beautiful, *"as distinguished from the moral or the useful"* (italics mine).

I cannot believe it is possible to create anything of aesthetic significance without moral value. The attempt to do so would make an implicit moral statement. To consider the beautiful aside from the moral is, to my mind, only possible as an intellectual exercise. It is like knowing Siamese twins by name and being well acquainted with their separate personalities. You can speak of them, you can speak to them, individually. But neither one is going anywhere without the other. So it is with beauty and goodness. How can that which is good not be beautiful? How can that which is not good be beautiful? Our perceptions of beauty and goodness radically inform our definitions of goodness and beauty. We are saved from becoming hopelessly confused between the two by our knowledge and pursuit of God. Having determined as best we can that a project has the potential to honor God, we may, indeed, pour heart and soul and might into the aesthetic *and* moral significance of the piece. In this way we serve art by lifting it to the highest plane within our theoretical and technical grasp so that it may be the most fully realized possible expression of intent.

This fullest possible realization of the intentions of a production's creators most fully serves the audience. What an extraordinary thing is an audience. In today's society, most of us have many obligations, so many that it is hard to fit them all into the day before dropping, exhausted, into our beds. We have many things to do, many things to think, many things to feel. Yet this remarkable *audience* sets aside all of this, sometimes at great sacrifice and expense, in order to present itself for engagement. The audience deliberately abandons other obligations and places itself before the actors in order to be compelled, to be transported, to be lifted out of—or into—self, and to go away refreshed, renewed, perhaps even fundamentally changed. When we honor God and serve the work, we have repeated chances to bring this gift to our fellows, who have come asking for it. One is awed.

It is fashionable in theatre companies to denigrate the audience. We speak of them as though they are crass and feebleminded—somehow not quite as bright or special as we ourselves. It is a form of humor, a way of releasing pressure. It is a harmless folly. Or is it? Think of the powerful exchange of energies that can take place between audience and actors in performance. Think of the trust that they bring to us as they set everything aside and come in anticipation. Think of the courage it takes for actors, night after night at eight, to say, "When shall we three meet again?," *knowing* all that must follow before the clock strikes eleven! Do we do our audience a disservice with our carelessly demeaning talk of them? Do we do ourselves a disservice? Art? God? It is so hard, but I want to remember Kierkegaard. I *believe,* and I want to *act as though I believe,* that what I say *matters*—that my attitude during blocking rehearsals affects the possibility for engagement of the woman in the third row on the left side on the second Thursday night of the run.

If our attitudes towards the audience matter, surely good will among the company is essential.

> Therefore, if you are offering your gift at the altar and there remember that your brother has something against you, leave your gift

> there in front of the altar. First go and be rec-
> onciled to your brother; then come and offer
> your gift (Matthew 5:23-24).

If I am telling myself that I am an actor for God's glory and in his service, I cannot ignore these verses. They are time consuming. They are no fun. They are necessary.

I had a friend a number of years ago who, when he met the Lord, had a firmly established habit of lying. Sometimes there was no reason. He would just open his mouth and out would come a lie. When he finally became ready to deal with this fault at any cost, he broke himself of it. He determined that every time he lied, he would confess it aloud to someone. A few painful incidences of honoring his word helped him to become conscious before he spoke, and he was able to form a new and more godly habit of speech.

Many of us have been in theatre longer than we have consciously been in the Lord. It is easy to pick up bad habits—habits of jealousy, lust, condescension or a critical spirit. If we want the power of God to flow unhindered through our acting, these spoiling habits have to go. It takes prayer, wisdom, and guidance from God daily to overcome mental habits that use others rather than honoring them. It isn't always best to confess to someone that you have spoken ill of them. Sometimes we only cause more hurt by easing our own conscience. Confess to God, with a determination to do what he requires to make the matter right. Ask him to restore favor and harmony between you and the other person and trust him to do it.

As far as lustful thoughts are concerned, we often take more blame than is ours. Some of these thoughts come from our flesh, but the enemy of our souls has a stronghold in this area in our society. Try this: when a lustful thought flits through your mind, immediately ask the Lord's help. Tell the lustful thought to depart. Then pray for the person involved for fifteen or twenty minutes. After a few such incidents, the enemy will stop bringing the person to your mind! This also works with movies, novels, or anywhere else you encounter attractive characters.

Servanthood is the natural flower of genuine community. To serve in love—to serve our fellow actors, the director, the prop person and the audience—all are the same action and are the ordinary behavior of the redeemed person. Generous, spontaneous service results in the last being first and the first being last, over and over and over. This is the natural order of things and, as we pursue our relationship with Christ, we find more and more joy in service.

I miss
you.
Come home
(cCU)
soon.

Love you
- ariel
:)

# THIRTEEN:
## Gifts of Self

*W*hen we give ourselves to people, we give them not only pieces of ourselves, but pieces of themselves—the pieces that wouldn't show up in any other mirror (just as each of us reflects something of God that wouldn't show up in any other mirror). All of us experience these gifts of knowing in our private lives. They come through time freely spent together, deliberately opening our hearts to one another in conversation and love.

In July of 2000 I spent several days in Snowmass, Colorado with a friend. She was going there for a medical seminar and would have a suite provided. She invited me to come for company and the fun of it. On one of her days off, we went to Maroon Bells.

Such a pretty name. There are posters of Maroon
Bells all over the place in restaurants and other
public areas in Colorado cities. I never thought I
would go there. It is a wilderness preserve outside
of Aspen, in the Colorado mountains. My friend's
little tour booklet contained pictures of wild life
one might see. I said to the Father that I would
like to see something, preferably a marmot, but if
not, it was o.k.

The drive there was pretty. It rained while we
were at the preserve, and the lightning and thunder
were lovely. There was a double rainbow, and the
mountains and water and foliage were beautiful.
After we had walked around, after the rain and
just before we left, I saw a couple of small birds
swooping and cavorting in the fresh, sweet air.
Here was my wild life. Thank you, Father. Then,
as we drove out, suddenly by the side of the road
a marmot scrambled to the top of a rock and sat
there boldly as we drove past! I wonder if he won-
dered why the Father had him scramble to the top
of a rock and sit there all exposed just when a car
was coming! How good that he obeyed. It makes

me want to be attentive to obeying His smallest promptings—He may be preparing a lovely gift for someone!

As Christians called to storytelling, we have the rare privilege of offering through our professional lives the same sort of gifts we offer in our deepest personal relationships. Certainly, acting is a craft with learnable skills. Learning the skills enhances the craft. But, beyond the craft, the stock in trade of theatre is empathy, conviction, grief, joy—things of the heart—the Things that Matter. There is only one gift, though it has a thousand, thousand forms. It is the gift God gave to us in Jesus. Made in His image, we give the gift to one another. The gift is self—the gift not only of knowing, but of being known.

When my son, Colin, was just fifteen, we had recently moved across country and he was in a new school. Our family was in grief because my husband—my children's father—had chosen to leave me the year before. We were all still very shaken. My daughter, Sasha, was in college in Colorado, and the boys and I moved to California, where we had old family friends and where I hoped new life patterns might help to heal our sorrow.

Colin was cast as the lead in his new school's spring play, a wonderful achievement. His character, Billy, was a boy whose fear of being unloved was so deep and overwhelming that he lost himself in a charming but desperate fantasy life.

Several weeks into rehearsals, Colin came home one evening and simply dissolved emotionally. "I can't do this," he wept. "When the other kids see Billy, they're going to know he's me and they're going to hate me!" We talked and prayed for a while. I assured Colin that, if he decided not to do the play, I would support him in that decision, as would his teacher—although it would probably mean she would have to cancel the performance. But I said more, too: "Colin, as an actor you have a gift to give. The gift is costly, and the level of vulnerability you will experience in giving it is not for cowards. Since you are *very* gifted, the cost is very high, and the potential gift is very valuable. It is true you have to expose your *self* to give this gift, and that experience can feel terrifying and humiliating. But I believe you are wrong about the response. Instead of seeing that Billy is you, and hating you for it, I believe they will see that Billy is them—for we are all Billy. They will feel less alone in their own Billy-ness, and they will love you for that."

Colin chose to take the risk, to sacrifice his hidden, inner privacy on behalf of his artistry. The show was wonderful, and Colin did, indeed, make new friends—a salve to his troubled soul in a difficult year of his life. Each of us faces the same battle on some level every time we bring a character to life—every time we choose to "make believe" instead of "pretend." It is the same battle I was fighting after more than forty years in the theatre when I found the way to allow the character of Mrs. Watts to weep brokenly on stage. Every time we win this battle—every time we sacrifice our hidden, inner pride to make a gift for the audience—we help to restore the community of humanity. That is because, when we succeed in dying to ourselves in this particular way, someone watching is freed from some degree of

"Billy-ness," and the response is love. Love is always a mirror image of God.

In theatre, though not always in our daily lives, the gift is often intentional. Prayer is one of the most versatile gifts we can offer. I pray during process that God's purposes will be realized among the production company—any company I am working with, whether or not it is Christian. At the university, we pray together before performances—as well as during rehearsals—that God will pour his mysteries through us in ways to bless his people (and we are all his people, even if some of us do not know it).

As Christians working in non-Christian companies, of course, our prayers are private. But much of the content can be similar: that the relationships among the company may be honoring to God and that the production may be to his glory. Added to that, in any situation, are the individual prayers for personal concerns as we come to know and love the people with whom we are working. In a way, these prayers are the personal gift we offer—the gift that lies in our hearts whether or not we are artists. Everyone, through love and caring, has opportunities in personal life to help others feel less alone, to restore community to people's aching, lonely hearts. As professional storytellers, we have the enormous privilege of extending that gift to tiny lofts and crowded auditoriums—to bring intimacy, thought, challenge, conviction, comfort—to people who choose to come, choose to open themselves to our artistry—people who will go away knowing us, though we may ever meet only a fraction of them.

I am careful of the stories I tell on stage. I want them to be true and to bring glory to the Lord, both in process and in product. Can I want less for my daily life?

"Do nothing out of selfish ambition or vain conceit, but in humility consider others better than yourselves" (Philippians 2:3).

How do we do that in theatre? First, we have to *intend* to do that. There will be many, many failings and fallings short, but if the intention is present, we grow. The students where I teach are remarkably successful in rejoicing with those who rejoice and weeping with those who weep—even over casting decisions! New students often come to me some time during the year and say, "The theatre program I came from is very different. There are favorites and cliques, and it is full of pettiness and backbiting. I feel so welcome here! I don't seem to be required to prove anything—I am accepted and supported. It's wonderful!" This situation is not a happy accident of chance; it is the result of serious work on the part of the students. It is not easy work, and I am proud of my students' growth, both spiritually and artistically.

"Considering others better" does not mean I have to try to talk myself into the proposition that you are a better actor than I am. "Considering others better" is not a qualitative judgment of the mind. It is an attitude of the heart and, when it is operating properly, it is surprisingly unimportant who is the better actor. To "consider you better" as a fellow actor, I will want to care as much about your life, your work, your audition, as I do about my own. In practical terms this may work out as praying with you, or lending you my favorite skirt for your audition because you love it and it looks great on you, or discussing your audition piece with you, *when asked,* or not offering you a brownie when I know you are dieting, or guarding my mouth so I don't speak carelessly of you when you are not present. These and a thousand other actions can be part of considering one another better.

I have drifted back and forth, here, between "personal" and "professional" gifts of self. They are the same for us. It is one of the breathtaking blessings and difficulties of our calling. The more we practice genuine vulnerability—on stage, in class or in our personal lives—the better we will become at it in all three places. If our transparency grows, personally or professionally, it grows in the other arena, too. It can't help it. As actors, we are the instrument, the medium of expression within our art. When God blesses the work of our hands, He also blesses our hands.

# FOURTEEN:
## Broken Wholeness

$\mathcal{A}$s far as I know, they still haven't found matching snowflakes. I think identical twins are one of God's jokes. Not an unkind joke—those proceed only from fallenness—but a rollicking, exuberant, joyful joke. Do you know any "identical" twins? When you meet them, they are indistinguishable. After a while, as you get to know them, you wonder how you were ever confused—they look so different! Looked at closely, twins are not much more alike than any other two people. For that matter, look at an ethnic group different from your own. "They" all "look alike"! Until we look closely. Considering the amazing variety of creation, and how different we are from, say, flowers, no two people look very different from each other until we look closely. We are meant to look closely. It is part of "enjoying God forever," as the Westminster Shorter Catechism has it—part of the fun.

One of the truly staggering facts about people is that *each* of us and *all* of us are made in the image of God. It is up to each of us and all of us to reflect that image, and we do. Being fallen, we reflect other images, too. In addition to being fallen we are broken. It is easy for us to think that being fallen *causes* being broken. But God actually seems to like brokenness. The Father sent the Son to show us how to do it right. Jesus was broken in every right way there is to be broken, but without falling.

Jesus didn't reflect God, because he is God. If you have seen Jesus, you have seen the Father. If you have seen me, you have only seen an image of God, and one that could use quite a little bit of glass cleaner at that. But it is an individual image of God. Each of us produces an individual image of God, and that is something to be cherished. But it isn't where we get our value. Our value comes from our being, just like God's value comes from his being. That is part of the *way* we are made in his image. We admire and praise God for the marvelous things he does.

But we are called to love him for himself, and that is the way he loves us. He is excited and pleased about our doings—the way I am excited and pleased when the girl in acting class finally remembers to cross left, or the boy in Shakespeare class remembers the meaning of "iambic pentameter." But God loves us absolutely free standing—just because. When Moses asked who God was, God said I AM, as though that explained everything. If you will allow, it does. We am, too. And that, too, explains everything.

Kathleen Norris, in *The Cloister Walk*, quotes Martin Buber speaking of a Rabbi Zusya, who is reported to have remarked, "In the world to come I shall not be asked: 'Why were you not Moses?' I shall be asked: 'Why were you not Zusya?'"

I want passionately to manage to *be* Sanne here and now so that I won't deserve that question. Being me is a highly individual matter, as is being you. The individuality pours, floods, cascades into our creativity, into our acting, if we will let it. That is why Branagh and Gibson can both play Hamlet, both play it truthfully, and why we want to see both and don't get bored.

It's like the meaning of words. Earlier I spoke of your bringing your entire life history to the meaning you give a word and my bringing my life history, too. Our two life histories, in our conversation, give nuances to the meanings of certain words that they will never have in any other conversation, because I am I and you are you.

It is the same with discovering a character. When you look at Linda Loman in *Death of a Salesman* and ask yourself what she wants, the answer comes not only from the text, but from your life experience. Because theatre is communal, the answer will also come from your director, and from the guys playing Willie and Biff and Happy—from their responses to you in rehearsal and performance.

The answers also come from our larger societies. One of the most fascinating progressions to trace is the performance of Shakespeare. Every great Shakespearean actor has been described as great because "he was so real!" Yet, a generation later, this work was seen as stilted and dull, while someone else's work was hailed as "real." When I was in school everyone was raving about Olivier.

Later, I found Branagh's work fresh and electric. Who will be next?

In callback auditions, I tell my students, "Callback auditions are not about whether you can act. If you couldn't act, you wouldn't be here. Callback auditions are about your height, hair color, the sound of your voice and a dozen other things you can't control. Because of them, you may not get to perform this role when the show opens. But you are here now, and we are here as your audience. You can perform the role now! Don't let anyone rob you of that opportunity. Have fun! Go for it! Take risks! Play the part!" We have a lot of fun at our callbacks. They are intense, exhausting, and sometimes long. But they are fun.

As actors, each character we play intersects with our own nature in such a way that the portrayal is both truthful and unique. Our worship intersects with the nature of God in much the same way, so that the image of God that each of us reflects is also truthful and unique.

Through theatre, through story—which exists only in the present, like eternity—we are able to craft images of God and of fallenness. Through these images, and through the communal process of creating them, we find our own wholeness and we invite others to wholeness. Inviting others to wholeness is the purpose of story. It is God's purpose in the Bible; it is Jesus' purpose in the parables, and it is our purpose. There is only one of you. You are the only one reflecting God from your precise perspective. This is true not only for your personal life, but for your professional life as a storyteller. No one else will ever play Hamlet, or Cinderella, or the Ghost of Christmas Yet to Come just like you. Only you can do it. So do it.

You are made in the image of God and you are unique. Is it o.k. for you to be an actor? If you are called to it, it is more than o.k. It is the doing meant to flow from your being, and your doing or not doing it will alter the universe.

6 con of trag: plot, theme, character, diction, music, spectacle

3 bib princ: 1- Art is within God's will - tabernacle revealed Go
  Value of design construction
  2- Artistic ability is God's gift - God placed ability t
  tabernacle in mens minds.
  3- Art is a vocation from God - calling

# Further Reading / Bibliography

Writers who have strongly encouraged my spiritual growth include Annie Dillard, Fenelon, Madame Guyon, Jo Kadlecek, Anne LaMott, Madeleine L'Engle, C.S. Lewis, and A.W. Tozer.

Writers who have strongly encouraged my theatrical development include Ama Ata Aidoo, Philip Auslander, Peter Brook, Jacques Derrida, Jerzy Grotowski, David Mamet, Wole Soyinka, and Ngugi wa Thiong'o.

I saw somewhere that "for relaxation" Madeleine L'Engle reads cellular biologists. I realized that I like to read about quantum physics.

Below are some specific references that might be difficult to just stumble upon:

*Stage by Stage: The Birth of Theatre*, Philip Freund. Peter Owen, London and Chester Springs.

*Ur-Drama: The Origins of Theatre*, E. T. Kirby. New York, New York University Press, 1975.

*Theater and Incarnation*, Max Harris. Wm. B. Eerdmans Publishing Co., 1990.

Rep painting : uses elements to create an image of a natural or concrete object

Abstr paint: uses elements to express ideas, feelings, or sensations. effects senses

All-at-onceness: has the quality of being entirely, simultaneously present. unlike sequential nature of literature or performing arts)

CPSIA information can be obtained at www.ICGtesting.com
Printed in the USA
LVOW11s2237061213

364249LV00001B/102/P